ROADS TO THE ISLES

TOM ATKINSON

ROADS TO THE ISLES

By

Tom Atkinson

LUATH PRESS LTD.
BARR, AYRSHIRE.

This is the second book in the Series
'Guides to Western Scotland'

First Edition 1983
Second Impression 1983
Second Edition 1984
Third Edition 1985
Fourth Edition 1986
Fifth Edition 1988
Revised Edition 1989
Reprinted 1990
Revised and Expanded Edition 1991
Revised Edition 1992

Other books in this Series are:-

South West Scotland, which covers the area from Dumfries to Ayr.

The Lonely Lands, which covers the area from Dumbarton to Campbeltown.

The Empty Lands, which covers the area from Ullapool to Cape Wrath, and from Bonar Bridge to John O' Groats and Bettyhiill.

Highways and Byways in Mull and Iona, which covers the two most accessible islands of the Inner Hebrides.

Grateful acknowledgements to Dr. Sorley MacLean for permission, freely given, for the quotation used in the Introduction, which is taken from one of his great poems in Gaelic.

CONTENTS

Introduction   Page   1

Summary of Tours   Page   8

Fort William, Morar and Mallaig   Page   12

Morvern   Page   33

Strontian, Acharacle & Moidart   Page   49

Ardnamurchan   Page   71

Spean Bidge, Invergarry, Loch Garry,
Loch Hourn   Page   94

Loch Cluanie, Glen Shiel, Glenelg, Eilean Donan,
Kyle of Lochalsh   Page   106

Stromeferry, Loch Carron, Kishorn, Applecross,
Shieldaig   Page   132

Torridon, Kinlochewe, Loch Maree, Gairloch,
Inverewe, Loch Broom, Ullapool   Page   151

IN THE HIGHLANDS..........

In the highlands, in the country places,
Where the old plain men have rosy faces,
And the young fair maidens
Quiet eyes;

Where essential silence chills and blesses,
And for ever in the hill-recesses
Her more lovely music
Broods and dies —

O to mount again where erst I haunted;
Where the old red hills are bird-enchanted,
And the low green meadows
Bright with sward;

And when even dies, the million-tinted,
And the night has come, and planets glinted,
Lo, the valley hollow
Lamp-bestarr'd!

O to dream, O to awake and wander
There, and with delight to take and render
Through the trance of silence,
Quiet breath!

Lo! for there, among the flowers and grasses,
Only the mightier movement sounds and passes;
Only winds and rivers,
Life and death.

R.L. Stevenson

INTRODUCTION

What a task! Each one of these delectable areas should have a guide book ten times longer than this one. Each is an enormous area to describe, full of obvious beauty and hidden delights, replete with history, laden with myths. There is the burden of old remembered wrongs and sorrows here: there is an ancient, embattled culture: there are long traditions besieged by alien invasion. There is romance and real poverty.

Today the myth of Highland Romance is carefully fostered, especially by those who hope to profit from it. In reality, Highland history is a bloody mish-mash of clan warfare, feuds and piracy -- **they** are the reality behind the myth.

The clan chiefs, for power and wealth, segregated their miserable followers from all the social and economic progress that was taking place in the rest of Scotland and indeed in the whole of western Europe. When the time came that those renegade chieftains could satisfy their extravagance by exchanging their swords for an English pension, they did not hesitate for one moment in deserting their clans and selling the lands they claimed -- falsely -- as their own.

Only then, when that 'parcel of rogues in a nation' -- to quote Robert Burns -- had been paid off, did peace come to the Highlands, even if it was, in all too many cases, the peace of death. The Highlands had for centuries been devastated, looted, and damned by one of the most appalling ruling classes in all of world history, and the price of their pleasures, and of their final treachery, is still being paid. That is the reality behind the romance of the Highlands.

But it is still, and will remain, an area of quite incomparable loveliness. It is a wholly fascinating region, fascinating to visit, fascinating to study.

Clearly, any guide book has to centre itself somewhere, and the first part of this one is centred on Fort William, and all the tours described run from there. But Fort William is hardly the centre of the area covered; indeed, it is at the edge. However, all the roads radiate from the town, and it is perhaps the most convenient place from which to tour the whole area described.

There is a lot of accommodation, of all qualities and prices, in Fort William. However, except perhaps for Morvern (and there is a good hotel at Loch Aline) there is also excellent accommodation along all the routes described, and if you don't fancy the bustle of Fort William, attractive though the town is, you will certainly not be disappointed at the standards of accommodation and Highland hospitality out in the countryside.

Starting, then, from Fort Willliam, the Roads to the Isles run west and north-west, out to Ardnamurchan Point standing defiant against the Atlantic roar. Out to Morvern, that vast empty triangle which once guarded the Sound of Mull. Out to Mallaig, the last outpost on the mainland, beyond which the Islands begin. And then once more from Fort William, north again, over the great rocky spine of the country, then back to the west coast, and north to Ullapool, another port from where the ships go to the Isles, another *Road To The Isles.*

Much of the area used to be in Argyll before that ancient county disappeared (according to the bureaucrats) in the last quite ludicrous re-organisation of local government.

In terms of climate, Argyll is blessed. It is laved by the waters of the Gulf Stream, and is warm and equable. It can also be wet. For an odd statistic, you might note that more palm trees grow in Argyll than in any other British county!

The name derives from Arachaidal or Ergadia, the Boundary of the Gaels, and there are very ancient links with Ireland. The original kingdom of Dalriada in northern Ireland was colonised from Argyll, but the tide then turned, and the Irish people, now called Scots, returned to Argyll -- Ergadia -- and established a Dalriada there. And if you think that is confusing enough, it is only the very beginning, the first faint dawn-light, of history.

It would be tedious even to outline the history of the area, with its long story of clan battles and see-sawing clan fortunes. This area endured such things more than most others. It happened to be the borderland between the great clans of the Campbells and the Macdonalds. It was also a border between the Presbyterian and Catholic religions -- still is, in fact -- and that, too, caused much misery. The holiday-maker of today will hardly care whether he is in Campbell or Macdonald country, or, except perhaps on Sundays, in a Catholic or a Presbyterian area. The same rules of welcome and hospitality will apply.

And all of this great area is empty -- empty of everything except scenery, that is, and that scenery is unquestionably the best in Scotland and arguably the finest in the whole world. Of course there are settlements here and there (no need to fear going without any creature comforts!). There is even a little industry at Loch Aline and the prospect of more in the hills above Strontian. And there is forestry. There is agriculture of course, here and there, and fish farming and even deer farming, although how long these will survive is still a question.

To the romantic sentimentalist it is the land of Bonny Prince Charlie and his foolish, doomed, heroic attempt to hold back the hands of time. To the realist it is the land where venal chiefs sold the birthright of their clansmen for English gold and then watched disdainfully as the Clearances (which began later and lasted longer here than elsewhere) emptied the straths and glens and left "nettles growing where once the children grew."

In all of this, it is a playground without parallel for the sailor, the walker, the climber and the simple holiday maker. There are vast arcs of white sand, washed by a gentle sea, which sing as you walk barefoot over them. There are thousand-foot cliffs and gentle strolls through quiet valleys and by murmuring burns. There are great passes which will tax the strongest walkers. There is colour and shape in those hills and sea lochs which make the Greek islands drab. I will show you a sight down the Ardnamurchan Peninsula which, on any sunny day, *must* be Tir-nan-Og, the Islands of the Blessed, the Islands of Eternal Youth.

There is much to interest the naturalist in this land, for both flora and fauna are notable. Inevitably, the flora and fauna reflect the use that man is making of the land and the sea, and what we look at today is not necessarily what our fathers saw, nor what our children will see.

That is especially true in the last few years, when vast conifer plantations have appeared on the bare hills. That particular change, and it will be a permanent change, inevitably alters the whole of nature around it. It seems that the forestry industry plants nothing but pine trees. I suppose there is a very good economic reason for this, since they grow quickly and in poor soil, but the visual effects can be appalling. The essence of Highland scenery is variety. Every hilltop and every corner gives a new and lovely view. If every view becomes a monotony of greenish-black conifers stretching to the horizon and beyond, then the whole character and nature of the area is changed. And certainly not for the better.

To be fair, it is the recent policy of the Forestry Commission (although not of all others) to plant a proportion of hardwoods at the edges of their vast conifer plantations. Eventually this will help, but only a little. It is about as effective as painting your own front door in a decrepit tower block.

Of course, once, long ago, these mountains were covered by great forests, but they were forests of oak and other native, mostly deciduous trees, not the pines of today. There are still some remnants, especially around Strontian, of those vast woodlands, and today they are carefully preserved. Then, the deer lived and thrived in the forests, feeding well on all the herbage of the forest floor. They cannot live in the forestry plantations, though. For one thing, they are fenced out of them, and for another, nothing grows in the deep shade of pine trees.

Still, for today at least, there of lots of deer in all this vast area, red, roe and fallow, and they are easy enough to see, if not to approach.

Of course, like the salmon and sea trout in the rivers and the brown trout in the hill lochs, they are protected and you must not think to shoot them. But you are in Scotland, and the law of trespass here is different and much more sensible than that of the rest of Britain, so you can wander at will, and when you will, over these hills. Do not, though, carry a gun or a rod, or you might then be charged with trespass in pursuit of game, and that is an offence, and a heinous one.

You will of course respect the farmers when you are walking, and not break down fences or gates. And you will, of course, use some discretion and sense in walking the hills during the shooting season, for there are high-powered rifles around then, and not all of them in skilled and responsible hands. It cannot be easy to mistake a walker for a deer, but it has happened.

As well as deer, there are wild cats here -- real ones, not feral domestic tabbies -- but you are unlikely to see one. There are seals, and those you will surely see. There are red squirrels and badgers and even a few, a very few, pole cats and pine martens. There are curlews, shags, oyster-catchers, lap-wings and ptarmigan and every possible sort of gull. There are ravens and owls and even eagles. There are hooded crows, and every farmer is a sworn enemy of every hooded crow, for that bird has the pernicious practice of attacking new-born and even partly-born lambs, and pecking out their eyes. And there are a few adders around, too, as well as grass snakes and lizards.

Long ago, when early Stone Age man first lived and hunted on the Scottish hills, there were reindeer, bear, wild pigs, moose, goats, lynx, wildcat, wolverines, otters, badgers, mink, pine marten, polecats, weasels and stoats to keep him company, and bones of all these have been found, together with the bones of the people themselves. But most of these animal species have long disappeared.

As for the flora, there is much more than the ever-present bracken and heather, although they are everywhere, and it is their colours which predominate on most hillsides. There is many another plant of the heath and moorland, and it is always interesting to examine very closely just one square yard of open hill, and see how many varieties of plant you can discover. It might be only twenty, but it might equally well be a hundred.

Of course, it is that vast variety of plants and herbs which makes Highland mutton and lamb so very delicious and different. It hasn't just been fed on grass alone, but on a hundred different plants, sweet and sour, aromatic, salty and spicy. No wonder it is different; no wonder it is incomparable.

On the higher and barer hills, there is a great display of alpine varieties, particularly of saxifrages and creeping azalea. And almost every rock outrop carries a most wonderful display of lichens, in colours and shades that would disgrace no gardener. These miniature natural gardens -- which may have taken a hundred years to grow (and which can be destroyed by one careless foot-step) -- are a great delight, and well repay the closest examination of their wonders.

However, you don't have to climb the hills to see most remarkable natural gardens. Go to the shore line and scramble around there. At one place in particular (although it is invidious to choose one amongst so many), by the sea-gate at Mingary Castle in Ardnamurchan, there is a most wonderful natural rock garden, just above the water line and washed often by sea spray. Crimson and pink sea-thrift flourish, and a great host of bright, colourful plants cling to that inhospitable rock. A most charming display indeed.

It must be admitted that not every day is sunny, and that there is not a great deal of indoor entertainment in this vast area. But the weather is a gamble anyway: you win some, you lose some. May and September tend to be the best months, and the midges, that curse of the Highlands, are not so active then.

Mountains and the sea and distant faery islands rising from a blue Atlantic. That is our area.

Comhlan bheanntan, stoiteachd bheanntan,
corr-lios bheanntan fasmhor,
Cruinneachadh mhullaichean, thulaichean, shleibhtean,
tighinn 'sa' bheucaich ghabhaidh.

A company of mountains, an upthrust of mountains,
a great garth of growing mountains,
a concourse of summits, of knolls, of hills
coming on with a fearsome roaring.'

That was how Sorley Maclean described such lovely places, and nothing could be more vivid or true.

So, let us begin with Fort William.

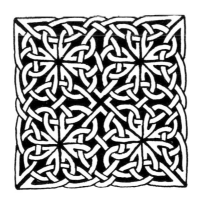

SUMMARY OF TOURS

TOUR ONE
MORAR
Fort William to Banavie, A82, (1 1/2 miles), Kinlocheil, A830, (10 miles), Glenfinnan (5 miles), Lochailort (14 miles), Arisaig (18 miles), Morar, Mallaig (9 miles). Return by the same roads. TOTAL: 95 miles.

This tour to Mallaig takes you through beautiful Glenfinnan with its National Trust Memorial to Prince Charles Edward (Bonny Prince Charlie) and the dead of the 1745 Jacobite Rising. It goes on to the sea at the Sound of Arisaig and then north to Mallaig. There are various recommended walks into the hills of South Morar, and a lovely side trip along the north side of Loch Morar.

TOUR TWO
MORVERN
Fort William to Corran Ferry, A82, crossing ferry to Ardgour, A861, (8 miles), Inversanda, Strontian (13 miles), Loch Aline, A823, (20 miles), Drimnin, B849, then return to Loch Aline and beyond to B8043, Kingairloch, Inversanda, A861, to Corran Ferry and Fort William (50 miles). TOTAL: 111 miles.

This tour takes you deep into the very remote and lonely district of Morvern. Apart from Loch Aline village, there are no stores or hotels in this whole vast area, so go prepared. The route takes you to a deer farm at Rahoy on Loch Teacuis, on past a sand mine and the interesting Kinlochaline Castle, right up the Sound of Mull, and even along the deserted south shore of Loch Sunart to the very lonely island of Oronsay and Loch Droma Buidhe. In returning, you take a minor road to the tiny settlement of Kingairloch, then back to Corran Ferry and Fort William.

TOUR THREE
MOIDART
Fort William to Corran Ferry and Ardgour, A82, (8 miles), Strontian and Salen, A861, (25 miles), Acharacle, Kinlochmoidart, Lochailort (21 miles), Glenfinnan, A830, (14 miles) and Fort William, (14 miles). TOTAL: 82 miles.

This is a most magnificent tour which travels a road recently opened in country where previously there was no road at all. It crosses Corran Ferry, and goes through Glen Tarbert to Strontian and Salen, along the shores of Loch Sunart. It then goes on to Acharacle, with a side trip to delightful Ardtoe. Another side trip takes you to the ancient Castle Tioram, seat of Clanranald, and then the main road continues on up the spectacular shore of Loch Ailort with its magnificent panorama of sea and islands. It joins the Mallaig road (see Tour One) at Lochailort for the return to Fort William. There are many suggested walks in the hills, and descriptions of other possible side trips to very delightful and lonely places, such as Loch Doilet.

TOUR FOUR
ARDNAMURCHAN
Fort William to Kinlocheil, A82 and A830, (12 miles), Ardgour, A861, (21 miles), Strontian and Salen (25 miles), Glenborrodale, B8007, and Kilchoan (19 miles), Ardnamurchan Point and Lighthouse (8 miles). Return by same road to Ardgour for Corran Ferry and Fort William. TOTAL: 158 miles.

This tour takes you to the farthest western point of the British mainland, the lonely and remote Ardnamurchan Point. It travels along the whole length of Loch Sunart, with beautiful vistas of islands, hills and trees. The ancient Mingary Castle, with its vivid memories of clan battles long ago, is visited. There are suggested side trips to the lovely sands at Sanna, and to the rock-bound northern coast of the Ardnamurchan Peninsula. Many delightful walks are suggested into the Sunart hills. The Lighthouse at Ardnamurchan is visited. Return to Fort William by the same lovely road to Corran Ferry.

It is reasonable in the first part of this book to describe some specific tours, and a summary of these is given above. North of Fort William, though, on the road northwards, there would be no point in recommending particular tours. There are various roads to take, and most are described, but the object is to go on northwards, not particularly to take circular tours.

Ann R. Thomas.

FORT WILLIAM, MORAR AND MALLAIG.

It is a pity that this whole noble land does not have a noble doorway, and whatever else it may be, Fort William is not noble. Just the same, it is not a bad little town, and certainly it is in a grand position on Loch Linnhe. Ben Nevis, very close to the town, is a most deceptive mountain, which never shows itself to advantage, even if it is the highest mountain in Britain. It is climbed easily enough from Fort William, through Glen Nevis, but the climb is a serious undertaking, even in the best of weather.

Fort William is a town closely geared to the presumed needs of the holiday maker, although far removed from the delights of, say, Blackpool. There are plenty of good hotels, and you can eat and drink well there. However, there is certainly a great deal of tartan and haggis frippery.

Surely the finest thing in Fort William is the West Highland Museum, right in the centre of town. It has not expanded much over the years, but is still small, friendly, interesting and helpful. There is a rebuilt 'black house' there, not cleaned up and sanitised, but kept as it must have been when it was lived in a hundred years ago. Most interesting, though, is the 'hidden portrait' of Prince Charles Edward -- the Bonny Prince Charlie of legend. The portrait is one of two known to have been painted, although the other has long since disappeared, and indeed the one in Fort William is said to have been rescued from a rubbish dump. The portrait itself is a seemingly meaningless daub of blotches, whirls and blobs of colour painted in a half circle on a board. However, when you put a polished metal cylinder on to the board, and look at the reflection in the metal, you see a miniature portrait of the Prince, dressed in a satin coat, with a

brown wig and wearing the Garter Star.

It is all rather eerie, and brings to mind those days when troops of redcoats ranged these hills, burning, killing and pillaging, helping to destroy for ever an ancient and anachronistic way of life, and when it was treason to possess a kilt or a gun, let alone a picture of the Prince.

There is nothing particularly old about Fort William, and it is even difficult to find traces of the Fort. That was originally built in 1615 by General Monk, of earth and sods. Later William III had it rebuilt in stone. Now it has just about all vanished.

Leave Fort William by the A82, signposted Inverness, and after about a mile, turn left on to the Mallaig road, A830. Nearby, where the river Lochy runs into Loch Linnhe, are the ruins of Inverlochy Castle. This is a very ancient place indeed, a place inhabited at least back to the 8th century. Being in the Highlands, it has a long history of violence. There was one notable battle there in the 15th century, and another in 1654, when Argyll attacked Montrose, who then held the castle. Argyll himself, though, took no chances personally. He awaited the result of the battle in a barge on the far side of Loch Linnhe. Perhaps he was wise, for his troops were well beaten.

The village of Corpach is 'The Place of Bodies'. The noble dead, from far to the north and the east, were carried to Corpach, there to await shipment by galley to the sacred Isle of Iona, for burial there.

Passing the ecological and economic excrescence of the Pulp Mill, another memorial to another futile effort to exploit the Highlands, you will soon be on the quiet shores of Loch Eil. Here is Achdalieu. In 1645, some 300 men, the garrison of Fort William, landed there to cut wood. The trees belonged to Sir Ewan Cameron of Locheil, and he, enraged at this plunder of his property, gathered his men and attacked the woodcutters. Locheil himself led the attack, and soon found himself locked in single combat with the officer commanding the English troops. Neither could gain the advantage, and soon, swords broken, they grappled with each other, and both fell into a ditch. Locheil, underneath, felt the enemy dagger at his ribs, but then, with his teeth, tore out the throat of his opponent. He is said to have remarked later that it was the sweetest bite he had ever had!

Of course, in those not so distant days, the Highlander was regarded with superstition and fear by the English and Lowland troops sent to occupy their land. It was even believed that the Highlanders had tails! It is strange to realise that the 'discovery' of the Highlands came several centuries after the 'discovery' of America! As knowledgeable Dr. Johnson wrote, late in the 18th century, after his tour of the Highlands: 'To the southern inhabitants of Scotland, the state of the mountains and islands is equally unknown with that of Borneo or Sumatra.'

From the head of Loch Eil, where a road (A861) branches off to the left and finally ends at distant Ardnamurchan, the A830 runs on through wonderful country to Glenfinnan. The view from Glenfinnan down the narrow length of Loch Sheil must be one of the most stirring in all of Scotland, with the great hills rising sheer from the loch a tapestry of colour in all seasons. But see them, if you can, in autumn, when the bracken is a hundred shades of red and the heather still faintly purple. Then you have the epitome, the essence, the very marrow, of all Highland Beauty.

Glenfinnan is the centre, and focus, of all the Bonny Prince Charlie sentimentalism. It is National Trust property now, though, and the tawdry is excluded. The National Trust has a Centre there, with a very good display and exhibition as well as a tea room, which might be welcome.

On a level, grassy field by the shore of the loch there is a monument, fittingly, to the men who fought and died in that daft and desperate, but eternally moving, rising of 1745. It was on that flat meadow where the monument now stands that the Prince waited with his handful of followers on August 19, 1745. He waited, and it seemed that none would come. Then, finally, over the hills came

Locheil and his men, pipes playing, and the Standard of white, blue
and red silk, was raised by the old and feeble Tullibardine.

Thus began a desperate venture whose ending in genocide and
doom some surely foresaw that day.

Later, much later, when the clans were scattered and a whole
society broken, after an ancient culture had been destroyed, the
monument we see today was raised by MacDonald of Glenaladale,
whose grandfather died at Culloden. Many of the stones came from
cairns built at Glenfinnan by men marching to war. Each laid a stone
on a cairn, and if he returned, each removed a stone; what was left
was a monument which the dead had raised to themselves. After the
'45, many cairns were left as they had been when the men marched
off.

No-one can be unmoved by Glenfinnan. Ghosts walk there,
and the past becomes the present. Roses, wild roses grow there.

Hugh MacDiarmid wrote:

> *The rose of all the world is not for me.*
> *I want, for my part,*
> *Only the little white rose of Scotland,*
> *That smells so sweet,*
> *And breaks the heart.*

Let us perhaps leave the last word to Queen Victoria, who visited Glenfinnan, and wrote in her diary: 'I never saw a lovelier or more romantic sight, or one which told its history so well. What a scene it must have been in 1745! and here was I, the descendant of the Stuarts and of the very King whom Prince Charles sought to overthrow, sitting and walking about quite privately and peaceably.'

There is a tiny unused graveyard in the field by the Monument. Probably the original name of Dalnaomh (Holy Field) came from this old burial ground. The quite large church at Glenfinnan stands between the road and the Loch, and it is attractive in its austerity. Another MacDonald of Glenaladale built the church in 1873, again in memory of the Prince. The bell was never hung in the bell-tower, because, legend says, MacDonald lost all his money at the crucial moment. He had invested in the Papal State and when Garibaldi united the Vatican State with Italy, Macdonald lost his investment. He is said to have remarked that he had only sixpence left, and that had the wrong head (Victoria's presumably) on it.

It is strange that MacDonald built such a large church for a population reduced by his own grandfather's clearance of peasants and smallholders from the land they had held down the centuries. They were shipped, ironically, to Prince Edward Island in Canada.

From Glenfinnan, the road to the west climbs the hill of Schlatach, then drops down to Loch Eilt, the Hinds Loch, through the very pleasant Glen Muidhe. The fresh-water Loch Eilt, famous for its seatrout, is quite delightful, cradled by great jagged hills of considerable grandeur, and studded with tiny pine clad islands. Just below the road is an ancient black oak tree, and it is said that Prince Charles Edward sheltered under its branches after Culloden.

For much of the way, the road and the single-track railway run together, but at Loch Eilt they separate, with the road sticking to the northern shore of the loch and the railway to the southern. Just beyond the point where the two separate is Creag Bhan, and from there a rough track, sometimes quite hard to follow, runs south to

Glenaladale, near Loch Shiel. It is not a track to be taken casually, but if you are equipped for it, then it takes you through country of rare beauty. But it is empty country, and hard, so do not go unprepared. It might be worth your while, though, for the buried treasure of Alisdair Oir (Alisdair of the Gold) still lies somewhere in the strath of Glenaladale.

Alisdair's instructions for finding the treasure are clear enough (just dig where seven rounded peaks can be seen), but none has yet located it. Four, even five, peaks are easy to see, but the others have still to be sighted. Perhaps it could be your lucky day!

At the western end of Loch Eilt, across and above the railway, is the strange, haunted Creagan an t-Sagairt, the Rocky Place of Priests. This is a rich and fertile plateau, up the hillside and quite invisible from below. There are several ruined crofts, and over all a peculiar sense of desolation and sadness. The sorrows of the evicted crofters seem very real here, and you can well imagine the keening as the roofs were torn off and the Canada-bound ship waited in Loch Ailort.

Just where the road and rail join again (the railway goes under the road), at the western end of Loch Eilt, is Arienskill. From there, a track runs north, up the hill, following the burn (Allt an Criche) towards Loch Beoriad. Keep right where the track forks, and in a short time you reach a band of trees running down the loch. Here is Prince Charles Edward's Cave. It is wide-mouthed and deep, and the Prince, with his few followers, is said to have spent three days and nights there when on the run after Culloden.

Then, two hundred and more years ago, these hills and glens and straths must have been well populated -- the ruined crofts tell their own story -- and the whereabouts of the Prince known to many. But not one of them informed, even though the reward of £30,000 was wealth unimaginable.

Since you have walked so far already, walk further on the same track, and follow the river Meoble to the tiny isolated community of Meoble. The English name comes from the Gaelic

Miath Pol, meaning 'Rich Soil', and the rich, alluvial flat, sheltered by wooded hills, lives up to its name.

Close by Meoble is the equally tiny settlement of Rifern, and Rifern is also the name of the fearful phantom grey dog of Meoble, whose appearance means a death in a certain MacDonald family. Long ago, in the days when anything could happen, and most things did, MacDonald of Rifern owned a great grey dog which was very attached to him, and very faithful. However, MacDonald had to go to war (perhaps the Campbells were being a nuisance again), and Rifern had to stay behind. She pined greatly for her master, and eventually ran away from home and settled on an islet in the Dubh Lochan. There she had a litter, and she raised all her pups successfully. They hunted together, and lived safely on the little island. After two years, MacDonald returned home and learned what had happened to his beloved Rifern. He went to the Dubh Lochan and swam over to the

PRINCE CHARLES EDWARD'S CAIRN, LOCH NAN UAMH

islet. Sadly, he got there when Rifern was off hunting on her own, and the strong young dogs attacked Mac-Donald and killed him. To this day, Rifern haunts those wooded hills, howling for her long dead master, and fore-telling death, whenever she appears, to the family that removed his body from the islet and buried it in the tiny overgrown cemetery where the track ends on the edge of Loch Morar.

From the shores of Loch Morar, you must go back the way you came, unless you have arranged for a boat to carry you down the Loch. Go further on the road, and you reach the sea at Loch Ailort.

For this tour, do not take the road turning left at Loch Ailort, which runs right down Loch Ailort and into Moidart. It is a road of unsurpassed glory, but keep it for another day. Instead, continue into Morar, by the road along the Sound of Arisaig (what glorious names these are in English, and in Gaelic they ring like a peal of bells!) and through the village of Arisaig, turning north there for Morar and Mallaig.

Just past Loch Ailort, the diamond-shaped peninsula of Ardnish separates Loch Ailort from Loch nan Uamh. Ardnish is another great place for walking, although only one real track crosses it, starting from Polnish on the main road. It is a rocky, hilly area, liberally endowed with delightful lochans in the hills, and with most wonderful views of distant mountains and islands sailing like swans on the blue Atlantic waters.

Raoghal Mor, a great piper, was born in Ardnish. Once, at a big gathering, he found his hands so cold that he could not finger his chanter. A dairymaid, surely herself accustomed to cold hands, advised him to rub his fingers with an icicle. He did that, and found he could then play, quite brilliantly, one of the most difficult pieces he knew. No piper could follow that act, and he received the award. Ever since, the piece he played has been known as Glas Mhear -- The Tune of Locked Fingers.

At the very edge of Ardnish is a tiny islet, Eillean a Chaolais, which shelters the little bay of Port Na H-Aifrinne, The Harbour of Masses. It was here that mass was celebrated in the old days, when it was the turn of the Protestants to repress the Catholics. Believers from as far away as Eigg came then to worship at Ardnish.

From Polnish, (where we diverted, on foot) to Ardnish, the road continues westward, crossing and recrossing the railway, and skirting the lovely Loch Nan Uamh -- Loch of the Caves. It was to this loch that Prince Charles Edward came from France in 1745, and it was from here that he left, defeated, in 1746.

On the shore of the loch, just before Arisaig is reached, the old Borrodale House once stood, and it was there that the Prince spent his first night on Scottish soil, having landed from the *Du Teillay* with his handful of followers. It was at Borrodale that the young Prince stayed for a week, conferring with and persuading the Clan chiefs, who were very unenthusiastic about his venture to gain the

throne of England as well as that of Scotland. Finally, he converted Donald Cameron of Locheil to his cause, and that was the turning point, for Locheil had great influence, and where he led, many others followed.

On 19th September, 1746, Charles and others boarded a French ship, *L'Heureux* there at Borrodale, and sailed away from Scotland, never to return, and ended his life in miserable debauchery. A cairn marks the spot where he embarked.

When he left Scotland, Borrodale House had already been burned by the avenging English (and Scottish) troops, and his last night in Scotland was spent in a cave. Although it is well hidden, you can still find the cave, just below Arisaig House, and to the right of the burn. It is sheltered by a mound, which is in fact the few remains of a vitrified fort.

These vitrified forts are very interesting, and there are several in this corner of Scotland. Actually, little is known of them. To be 'vitrified', of course, is to be turned into glass, and that is just what has happened. Clearly, the forts, or strong houses, were constructed of rough, silaca-bearing stones embedded in brush wood. Somehow, whether accidentally or deliberately or by enemy action, the brushwood has been fired, and the resulting great heat has fused all the stones together and vitrified them into one great glass palace. It was all a very long time ago, of course, and even glass palaces weather and age, so that little is left of this one, or of the several others.

On westwards again to Arisaig, and a narrow, twisting road from the village will take you into the Rhu of Arisaig. Not perhaps a road for the faint-hearted, but very much worthwhile. It winds westwards at first along the shore of Loch Nan Ceallt before turning south to Rhu House. It is wholly delightful on a summer evening, as the sun shines on a myriad islands and as seals flop on the rocky shores.

You can also reach Rhu House by a foot track leaving the main road just by Arisaig House. This track takes you by the Ridge of Oak Trees and the Hill of the White Ox. Both oak trees and white oxen were important in the ceremonies of the ancient Druid religion, and near those hills is a great stone engraved with the mysterious, ancient 'cup and ring' marks. The juxtaposition of these ancient names and the incised rock are strong evidence that cup and ring

marks, wherever they occur (and they are common enough in Scotland) are related to that obscure and perplexing Druidical religion of old.

The track passes by the tiny, jewelled Loch nan Eala. Long ago, the Loch was much bigger than it is today, and it contained a 'crannog'. (A crannog was a fortification actually built on piles driven into the bed of a loch, and approached only by one, usually zig-zag and easily defended, track.) When the Loch shrank, for whatever reason that happened, this crannog was left high and dry, and its remnants can still be seen to the south of the Loch. Nearby, some Clanranald chieftain built a small castle in 1700, but nothing of that remains. Strange that the crannog, certainly more than 2000 years old, can still be seen, while the castle, not three hundred years old, has vanished.

Back, then to the main road at Arisaig and Keppoch. The old church at Keppoch was built in the 15th century by the 12th Chief of Locheil. It was one of seven churches built by him as a penance for his practice of torturing cats! There is an obscure legend that he was caught at this dreadful hobby one day by the Devil himself, in the shape of a great black cat, attracted by the screams of Locheil's victims. The Devil imposed the penance of building seven churches. It all seems somewhat unlikely.

In the churchyard, among several stones carved on the sacred island of Iona, is the grave of the 9th Chief of Clanranald, murdered by his stepmother. Really, the Highland chiefs were a most peculiar bunch, of unwholesome habits even before they were seduced by English gold.

Around Keppoch the rash of caravan parks is somewhat unsightly, if inevitable. No chance, on this gale-lashed coast, of screening caravans by a belt of trees. There is a golf course ('links' is a better word) here too, and it is perhaps unsurpassed for the beauty of its surroundings. Play it, by all means, but you will certainly find your score badly affected by the views. And perhaps by the wind.

Just by Keppoch, between the Hill of the Englishman and the Hill of the Scotsman, there used to be a croft where the last recorded kelpie found its last recorded victim. A kelpie, of course, is a water horse, a sprite that drags its victims into lochs and drowns them. Two sisters, orphans, lived alone in the croft, and one stormy night they were visited by an old wandering woman, seeking shelter from the gale and the rain. The old woman was made welcome, but in the night she stole away one of the girls and drowned her in a lochan.

The old woman was a kelpie, of course, and had the girls been older they would have recognised her by her hooves, and they might even have bridled her, for when the kelpie is in human form it is fairly defenceless. But when it is in the form of a horse, nothing is stronger, nor more beautiful and tempting.

If you should by chance see a beautiful white stallion resting by the side of a lochan in these hills, do not be tempted to ride it, however gentle it may seem. It will be a kelpie, and the moment you mount it, it will be off into the lochan, and you will be seen no more.

Just past Traigh House there is a cave, and in that cave there once lived a headless woman. She is gone now, but her head is still hereabouts, and one day she will return for it. She was a poor woman, and was unlucky enough to be caught stealing corn from the fields of Traigh House. In his anger, the laird cut off her head with his scythe. From that time, she, Colann Gunn Cheann (The Headless Body), lived in that cave, appearing every harvest time to disrupt the reaping. And no doubt to haunt the laird. Eventually she was banished to Skye by a man who fought against her, but she will return one day, when the harvest is ripe, for her head, and for her revenge.

The road turns north at Arisaig, heading directly for Mallaig. But if you go straight to Mallaig, then you will miss the delights of Loch Morar, and those delights are many. Twenty miles long and perhaps a thousand feet deep, Loch Morar runs far into the lovely hills, dividing north and south Morar. The very appropriate Gaelic name is Mor Dobhar -- Big Water. Today, the English name, Morar, is given to the whole area.

The freshwater loch is very deep, and is said to be the second deepest body of fresh water in Europe, and yet only one mile separates it from the sea. Even on the brightest day, Loch Morar is a mysterious place, and well repays exploration on the tracks which pass along the northern shore. The southern shore is almost entirely trackless, but rudimentary roads and tracks follow the northern shore for some miles to Tarbert, where only a narrow neck of land divides Loch Morar and remote Loch Nevis.

As always, 'Tarbert' means a place where boats were dragged overland to avoid a long and dangerous sea journey. And it **would** have been a dangerous journey, too, from the Morar river round the Mallaig headland and into Loch Nevis.

You can get a first taste of the beauty of Loch Morar on the road leading from Morar village past the church and Morar Lodge. The whole western end of the Loch opens up to you, lovely and island-studded. And the further you go, the more beauties appear. If you travel that road by car, or, better, by foot, you will almost certainly have it all to yourself, and be able to enjoy scenery of a very rare order.

Just above the pier on the road to Morar Lodge is a rock in the woods. This is the terrible Cairn Na Muic Dubh -- The Rock of the Black Pig. That was where a fearsome animal, half pig and half horse, lived and terrorised the countryside. Red-headed Alistair of the Crag, a bonny fighter, tried to kill it, but failed, and it injured him badly. Iain Dubh and Alan Mor (Black John and Big Alan, and who would want to face those doughty characters with names like that?) decided to do what Alistair had failed to do. Incidentally, all this took place not so long ago, for had not Iain's father himself been out in the '45? His father's spirit was not in Iain, though, for when the Black Pig appeared in all its ferocity, Iain took to his heels and the beast after him. There were some fearful screams from further down the Loch, and then silence. Alan decided, and who could blame him, to give up and go home and break the tragic news to Iain's wife. As he was doing that sad duty, who should appear but Iain himself, torn and bruised but safe. He would not, or could not, say what had happened, but the Black Pig has been seen no more. I wonder where these tales come from?

Another tale, of course, is of the Loch Morar mermaid. She was last seen in 1948, or, rather, the last publicised reports of her being seen were in 1948. This Mhorag is herself a death warning to a certain family, who well know the story of Mhorag, but who do not wish to be known themselves. Not so very long ago, the Mhorag appeared to a whole boatload of passengers on the Loch. She raised herself high out of the water (and that must have been a sight for the staid Highlandmen) and shook her golden hair. Gold coins flew out of her hair in all directions, like drops of water, and many fell into the boat. So unless you belong to that particular benighted family, keep your eyes open: you might be lucky.

FALLS OF MORAR

Whether you are on foot (which is much the best) or driving on this track, you pass derelict croft after derelict croft. Sad reminders, these, of a sad time when the people were driven from their homes so that sheep could graze the fertile glens and straths. And now the sheep have gone, and the hills are empty, and the descendants of the old loyal clansmen live, many of them, in Canada. And in Canada they all know the mysterious, anonymous Canadian Boat Song:

When the bold kindred in the time long vanished,
Conquered the soil and fortified the keep,
No seer foretold the children would be banished
That a degenerate lord might boast his sheep.

Better, perhaps, to boast his sheep than his deer forest, those sterile miles of desolation and sadness. But neither sheep nor deer need people, and what these glens and straths need, above all, is people, to bring back again the fertility and the richness.

Tarbert, which really is the end of the track, was once quite a bustling little place, bigger than Mallaig. Now it is dead, dreaming of what might have been had the railway come here instead of going to Mallaig. And it might well have done.

If you came on foot to Tarbert, then you can travel to Inverie by ferry, and on to Mallaig. Otherwise, you must go back by the track you came. Before you do so, though, you might care to walk along to Cnoc a Bhac Fhalaichte -- The Hill of the Bank of Hiding. It was here that a Tarbert man once hid his money, and died before he could dig it up again. Look in the burn, for several silver coins of the Stewart period have been found there in recent years.

On then, the last mile or two to Mallaig. Now that is a curious little town, which still seems strangely like an American frontier town -- a Highland Dodge City, perhaps. Until the railway came here in 1901, Mallaig hardly existed, being just a few crofts huddling between the steep ground and the sea. It was a lost community, unknown almost, approached only by 40 miles of rough track from Fort William. But when the railway came, there was direct and quick

MALLAIG

communication to Billingsgate and other southern markets, and Mallaig really boomed.

It is a ludicrous position, really, for any town, squeezed hard between the railway and the hills, and the railway owned the only bit of flat ground. However, it grew with the fishing, and even today, with the fishing itself in some decline, it is still one of the main ports for the Hebrides. You can join the intricate web of MacBraynes steamers in Mallaig, for the endlessly fascinating island-hopping voyages, or for travelling to the Isles. Smaller boats also sail from here, for various trips, including the passage to Rhum.

A great kippering factory was built at Mallaig (and what glorious kippers they made there, oak-smoked, from the plump Minch herring -- you can still buy them), and an ice factory, and fishing fleets from both east and west coasts berthed there.

Between the railway and the sea, in the old days, was Chinatown, a slum of wooden huts where the transient fisher-lassies, who cleaned and gutted and salted the herring, and followed the fleet as the shoals moved up and down and round the coasts, lived in their chaste squalor. Now, as the catch declines, the fishing boats disappear.

Just the same, Mallaig is still a major fishing port, even if the great days are gone. To see the fleet coming into harbour on a Friday afternoon is a great pleasure, and one which never palls. Mallaig shares with all fishing ports that remarkable sense of open-ness, that amalgam of land and water, that makes them so fascinating, especially perhaps to those for whom the sea is strange and rather frightening. The fishing may be in decline, relatively, but the fascination continues, and it is there in full measure at Mallaig, the end of the Road to the Isles.

There is not, perhaps, a great deal to detain the casual visitor to Mallaig, but you could well improve the shining hour by walking round the bay to the east, to the little village of Mallaigvaig. Prince Charles Edward landed there on his escape from Skye on 5th July, 1746. Climb any of the small hills around the village, and you will be rewarded by wonderful views of sea and sky and islands. The view stretches from Ardnamurchan to the Cuillins of Skye, and to far Kintail. Lovely, and quite unforgettable. Of course, from Mallaig, you must return the way you came, for Mallaig really is the end of the road. But surely it is no hardship to traverse again those forty miles of beauty and romance back to Fort William.

Decoration from 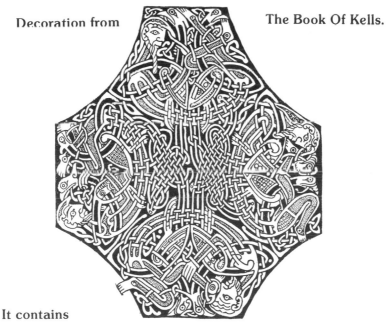 The Book Of Kells.

It contains
four men and eight birds,
intertwined.

Ann R. Thomas.

MORVERN

Morvern is an area, not one place. It is the great peninsula of land bounded by Loch Linnhe, the Sound of Mull and Loch Sunart. There are 275 square miles in Morvern, and it is nearly all empty and roadless. Our journey will take us to Loch Aline and beyond. Indeed, you can walk on hill tracks for miles beyond the last settlement at Drimnin, right round Auliston Point and along Loch Sunart to Loch na Droma Buidhe.

Of course, as usual in this part of Scotland, you must return the way you went: there are no circular tours.

Some hundreds of years ago, Morvern was heavily wooded, cloaked in deciduous trees which perpetuated themselves by self-seeding. Man intervened, though, and the vast forests were cut down to feed the primitive iron furnace at Lorne, across Loch Linnhe. The thin soil covering soon washed away off the hills when the trees were cut, leaving the bare and beautiful bones of the land for us to see today.

This time, leave Fort William by the main road south, the A82, to Corran Ferry. You have a long trip ahead, and it is worth taking the ferry to avoid the long road journey round Loch Eil. Not that there is anything wrong with that Loch Eil road. Indeed, it is very attractive, and it is dealt with in some detail in a later tour. Turn right off the main road at Corran, about 8 miles south of Fort William, and cross Loch Linnhe on the ferry. The ferry trip is always interesting, even if rather expensive these days. Looking down the long and narrow Loch, with hills on both sides, Lismore, 'the green and fertile isle' is in the distance. The great hills and long extinct volcanoes of Ardgour, Sunart and Morvern are on your right and the mainland, with the towering mountains of the Glencoe range, on the left. Up the Loch is Fort William, dominated by the bulk of Ben Nevis.

Although so massive, Ben Nevis is not an easy mountain to admire. Somehow, it always seems to blend into the background, and is inconspicious in spite of its great height and bulk. This view of it from the Corran Ferry is one of the best. Really to appreciate Ben Nevis, though, you need to climb it. It is the great ruin of an old volcano, founded on red sandstone. The central massif is a cone of volcanic rock 2000 feet thick, protected by belts of granite. The top of the mountain is a desolation of rock waste, bleak and frightening.

On leaving the ferry at Ardgour, turn left on to the A861 for Strontian. Just by the ferry is the lighthouse marking the Corran narrows. It was built in the early 19th century at the same time as the old jetty, now disused. Thomas Telford built that, in 1815.

The road runs quietly for about three miles along the shores of Loch Linnhe. At least, it runs quietly enough these days. Only a very few years ago the road was very narrow indeed, squeezed between the Red Rocks and the sea, and having some very difficult stretches. Now it is double width, and you can speed along, but if you do you will miss some fine glimpses of the great glens and corries of Ardgour. You might also form an intimate acquaintance with a highland cow, for they wander these hills freely, and are quite prepared to argue the right of way with any vehicle.

And speaking of cows, you might already have noticed that here in the Highlands there are very few of the big black and white Friesian cows that today supply most of our milk. Those Friesians simply are not tough enough to live on these hills. They are, in fact, nothing but perambulating milk factories (and poor watery stuff it is) and they need to be watched over and cossetted like fancy poodles. The cattle on these hills need to be tough and self-sufficient. Not for them the warmth and comfort of 'cow kennels' on winter nights and the expensive services of a vet. to help them calve. They face the winter gales with little in their bellies but a few heather shoots, and produce their calves unaided in some little hollow.

This is beef country, of course, and you will see several different beef breeds -- white-faced red Herefords, black Galloways whose hide is so thick and insulating they they will have unmelted snow on their backs three days after the last fall, and the majestic Highlanders. These last are the shaggy-coated red beauties with the great sweep of horn. They are very hardy and live out on the hills, and live off the hills, all the year round. Their long coats drain water off their bodies and their long forelocks or *dossans* keep their eyes clear of snow.

Highland cattle in a herd are quiet and picturesque and you might even think they look a bit dopey. Never, though, get between a Highland cow and her calf, or else you will see half a ton of beef on the hoof moving with tremendous speed and ferocity, and you will be the target for those horns.

It is also these quiet beasts, and these alone, which perform the peculiar Dance of the Highland Cattle, which is rarely seen, but always forecasts a great storm. They will assemble in a circle and one after another, in order of seniority, cavort and dance round the ring, each seeming to strive to outdo the rest in turnings and leaps and speed. Strange animals indeed, and they seem to have descended unchanged through many centuries. Indeed, they could be one of the original aboriginal cattle of Scotland.

You will perhaps notice, too, that the sheep hereabouts are almost all the hardy blackfaced variety. Like the cattle, they live out all the year round and scratch a very meagre living. Yet they do live, and they produce lambs, in conditions that would kill off the softer lowland sheep in a week. Of course, it is a matter here of acres to a sheep, not of sheep to the acre, and any farmer who gets one hundred lambs from one hundred ewes is both skilful and lucky -- a hundred and eighty lambs to a hundred ewes is common on softer land.

Like the Highland cow, the blackfaced sheep is naturally weatherproofed. Their wool is coarse and hard, considered unsuitable today for everything except carpets, but that coarse wool enables them to live and thrive in most inhospitable places.

But let us return to our tour. After three miles or so the road branches at Inversanda, with the left hand fork (B8043) continuing round the Loch and over the hills to Kingairloch. This present tour returns to Fort William by that road. For now, continue on the main road and climb up through Glen Tarbert.

The road remains open and fast, if you wish, but down to your left you will see the remains of the old road, and can perhaps envisage its delights and dangers.

Glen Tarbert (another place where boats were dragged overland to avoid a long and dangerous sea passage) is often gloomy. It is dominated by the great cliffs, ridges and precipices of Garbh Beinn (2903 feet) to the south. Often, torrents of water fall down those cliffs, to be torn to spray before they reach the bottom. There is wonderful climbing on those cliffs and very spectacular walking along the ridges, but only for those well-shod and prepared. Red deer roam these hills, and can often be seen grazing on the lower slopes. The roaring of rutting stags here, in this desolation, at the close of a winter day, is a mournful and wonderful thing to hear.

At the top of Glen Tarbert, just as the road begins to drop down, you can catch a first glimpse of Loch Sunart, Morvern and Ardnamurchan. The Carnoch River, running by the road and fed by a multitude of streams from the hills, begins to widen and run more peacefully as you approach the head of Loch Sunart.

Just before the river actually enters the Loch, a road to the left, (A884) crosses a bridge and carries on round to the south of Loch Sunart. The A861 continues straight on to Strontian and the delights of Ardnamurchan. Today, turn left for Morvern.

The A884 is a grand road with the Loch on your right, steep hills ahead and glorious views of Ardnamurchan. Where the road swings away from the Loch and climbs steeply into the hills a minor dead-end road continues along the side of the Loch. This leads to to Laudale and Glencripesdale, where there is an excellent small hotel, surely the most isolated in Scotland.

The A884, though, climbs steeply into the hills, and you are now travelling deep into the loneliness and all the loveliness of Morvern.

The name comes from the Gaelic, of course, and was originally *A Mhorbhaim,* which means The Sea Gap, and refers to the Sound of Mull. The Sound was once a very important sea passage, and also a boundary between kingdoms.

After its long steep climb, the road drops down into a valley, and a road to the left (B8043) leads back to Kingairloch. For now, though, continue on the main road towards Loch Aline.

There is an unclassified road to the right, leading to Rahoy, just after crossing the bridge over the river Aline at Claggan. 'Aline' by the way, means 'beautiful', a well-deserved name for the river and for the Loch itself. Take that unclassified road and head into the hills.

The road runs north-west by quiet Loch Arienas and between vast lonely hills to the shores of Loch Teacuis, a strange sea loch. Teacuis is narrow, long and shallow, and almost, but not quite, land-locked. It is part of an unusual geological fault running from Loch Sunart, through Lochs Teacuis and Arienas and out again to the sea by Loch Aline. A little more geological shaking and Morvern will be an island.

Go far enough along this roughish road and you reach Rahoy. Until recently there was a deer farm here, an experimental effort by the Highlands and Islands Development Board, and it was quite fascinating. Naturally, we think of the red deer as being a very shy, nervous creature, very afraid of man, and having good reason to be. Here at Rahoy the deer became so tame, in just one generation, that they queued up to have their ears scratched and would spend happy minutes sucking a finger. And there were not a few of them, but hundreds, and the calves especially were very loveable. Of course, you did not mingle with the antlered stags.

Not so long ago I asked one of the herdsmen how they managed to gather the herd off the hill when they had to be examined or treated or culled. I had memories of gathering sheep off hills like these, where men and dogs exhausted themselves whenever the flock had to be gathered. But how do you gather deer, which can outrun the swiftest dog? "Simple," he said. "Go up the hill with a bucket of nuts, rattle them, and run like hell to get to the pen before the deer can. They like nuts so much you can do anything with them." I wish sheep had the same liking!

Beyond the deer farm there is a very isolated Forestry Commission plantation of 2000 acres. There are some fine holiday chalets hereabout, and they must be the ultimate in 'getting away from it all'.

As usual, you must retrace your steps to the main road and go on, down the valley of the Aline, which flows from Loch Arienas, towards Loch Aline. You pass Larachbeg, where most of the people from St. Kilda were housed in 1930, when that distant island was finally cleared of people. They worked on forestry, but found it very hard to settle and to give up their unique, very democratic way of life.

Loch Aline village hardly lives up to its name. It is really not very beautiful, although its position is.

There is, surprisingly, some industry here, the only industry for many miles. A very special silica sand is mined at Loch Aline, sixty to seventy thousand tons of it every year. It is said to be the best sand in Europe for making the finest optical glass. Still, if you have to work in a sandmine, perhaps Loch Aline is the best place to do it.

The village is very finely placed, where Loch Aline itself opens into the Sound of Mull. A car ferry from Mull docks here, and is an alternative, albeit expensive, way of reaching Morvern. You take the ferry from Oban to Mull, and then a second ferry from Mull to Morvern. A bigger advantage of that ferry between Morvern and Mull, though, is that holiday makers almost anywhere in the area covered by this section of this book can take their car to Mull for a glorious day exploring that island, and still be back in time for dinner.

Before you reach Loch Aline village, though, travelling by road, you pass the dramatic Kinlochaline Castle, where the river enters the Loch. It was partially restored in 1890, and now consists of a four storey keep, with the walls ten feet thick. There is now a stone staircase to the entrance on the first floor, and this replaces the old wooden stairway, which could quickly be demolished when attack threatened. Note the gap in the walls above the gateway, from where various kinds of unpleasantness could be dropped on unwelcome visitors, and note, too, the nearby fireplace on the parapet where the unpleasantness could be boiled.

There is a stairway and various passages in the thickness of the walls, and these are difficult to understand, for they are very low and seem to lead nowhere in particular. Of course, no castle was complete without a dungeon, and there is a singularly nasty one here, in the cellar.

Built originally in the 14th century by MacInnes, Bowmen to the Lord of the Isles, it was burned down by the ferocious Colkitto MacDonald, Montrose's henchman, in 1644, and the present building probably dates from that time.

Locally, it is known as Casteall an-Ime, or Butter Castle. It is said that the men who built the castle originally were paid in butter! It seems most unlikely: more probably the rent was paid in butter, which was not unusual.

An ancient stone circle still stands between the castle ruins and the road. It must have seen some exciting events in its long history.

If you want to look over the castle -- and it is very much worth while -- enquire for the key from the caretaker who lives in the nearby cottage.

The big house seen through the trees is Ardtornish, a place, for me at least, permanently marked by the stigma of its association with the egregious Patrick Sellar and the viciousness of the Clearances.

Four miles down a track past Ardtornish, on a headland jutting out into the Sound of Mull, is the ruin of Ardtornish Castle. Little of it remains today, although enough to show the massive walls, still a landmark for sailors in the Sound. It, too was built in the 14th century, and was a very important stronghold of the Lords of the Isles. Sir Walter Scott, in his novel *Lord Of The Isles* based much of his highly romanticised story on Ardtornish, but in truth the Castle had a fairly quiet life.

The Lords of the Isles often sat in Council at Ardtornish Castle, and persistent legend holds that Edward I of England once visited the Castle to seek the help of the Lord of the Isles in his constant battle to impose English rule over Scotland.

Although Sir Walter Scott played fast and loose with history in his tales, he certainly wrote exciting stories, and standing in the sorry ruins of Ardtornish Castle today, you can almost hear again the music and singing as the Maid of Lorne prepares for her wedding; you can imagine the wind roaring through the rigging as the foundering ship of Robert and Edward Bruce fights its way into the bay; you can almost feel the excitement as the thousand oars of Lord Ronald's galleys beat their way down the Sound. It may not be history, but it is a wonderful story.

This area of Ardtornish is interesting to the geologist. There is a large and unusual outcrop of sedimentary rock underlying the district, and consequently the land is rich and fertile at least in contrast to the austerity elsewhere in Morvern.

Ardtonish, because of this fertile soil, supports a good deal of natural deciduous woodland, hazel scrub, and a very rich flora.

There is perhaps little to detain anyone in the village of Loch Aline itself, although there is an hotel there for refreshments, and a craft shop selling glassware made from the Loch Aline sand.

Continue then on the B849 for Drimnin. This is a delightful run, with the narrow Sound of Mull on the left and the hills of Morvern on the right, and with deserted little white sand beaches. The parish church stands about half a mile from the village on this road. The modern building is pleasant enough, but it replaced an older one in 1898, and the older one, built a century earlier, replaced one even older, although whether that oldest church was the original, founded by Columba himself, is not clear.

What is quite clear is that this was a very important centre of early Christianity in Scotland. Eithne, mother of Columba, was buried somewhere hereabout, but her grave is now lost.

The church houses a very fine collection of old grave stones, taken from the kirkyard. Most quite clearly come from Iona, and bear the typical carvings of swords and galleys, with intricate interlacing Celtic decorations.

Outside, still facing the elements, is the famous Morvern Cross, of lovely blue-green schist, tall and slender, and still on its plinth.

About two miles past the church, you enter Fiunary. This is the famous -- or infamous -- Fiunary of the song, that great lament of those cleared from their land and forced to emigrate to distant lands so that sheep could graze their parks.

No district in all of Scotland suffered more than Morvern in the clearances, and wherever you walk in those empty hills and along those empty shores, you will find old croft houses and the pathetic remains of the once fertile land now sour and unkempt.

The notorious Patrick Sellar was responsible for many of the Morvern clearances. Sellar, a lawyer, well earned his notoriety by his actions in leading and directing the clearances in Sutherland, for the Duchess of Sutherland. It was he who was responsible for evicting one old woman of Strathnaver, who was carried out of her house as it was fired. She died a few days later, and Sellar was charged with murder, and with various offences against property. To the surprise of no-one, he was acquitted by the unanimous verdict of his peers.

That was in 1816, and in 1838 Sellar, by then a rich man, bought his first land in Morvern. His first action was to have a flock of his sheep driven down from Sutherland, and to accomodate them, forty-four families -- 230 people -- were evicted. Within a few years, Sellar owned or rented 32,000 acres of Morvern, and occupied Ardtornish House.

No doubt he was a competent farmer, and equally no doubt he was a very heartless creature, whose *laissez faire* doctrine brought untold misery to many people, and wealth to himself.

His children were perhaps the first of the new generations of Highland landowners, who had a misty, sentimental attachment to their vast holdings, but who treated that land merely as a summer playground (and a source of considerable income and capital gain). They shot and they fished and they sailed their great yachts in and around Loch Aline and the Sound of Mull, but their real interests were elsewhere, and they played at being Highland Lairds. The great estates were run for them by their employees.

There was some competition as well as opposition to the Morvern Clearances. Some small farmers organised themselves into 'Club Farms' in which the animal stocks were held in common, and the arable land farmed privately. These Club Farms were quite successful, but were greatly disliked by the landowners. Sellar deliberately bought the land of Acharn, where there was one such Club Farm, and immediately evicted the tenants.

Even the unpromising land on the island of Oronsay, in Loch Sunart, was farmed communally in this way by tenants evicted by the Gordons from land at Auliston. A population of over fifty people lived on Oronsay, supported by a herd of cattle, and they prospered for over 25 years, until Lady Gordon had them evicted in 1868, in the last of the major clearances.

That was one particular victory which the landlords regretted. It happened that John MacDonald had lived as a child on Oronsay, where his father, until his early death, was a member of the Club Farm. The widow and the children left for Glasgow, but little John never forgot his roots, and during the Land League agitation of the 1880's, John MacDonald was a prominent leader in seeking some form of secure tenure for the Highland crofter. His evidence to the Royal Commission in 1883 was a bitter and biting indictment of what had happened in Morvern.

Today, reformist historians tell us that the Clearances were really not too bad, that they removed surplus population from a miserable existence in an anachronistic economy and gave them a chance of a new existence in a brave new world. Reformist historians always reflect the political flavour of the month, and these are no exception. In fact, the pre-Clearance society and economy of the Highlands was healthy and well-balanced, ecologically sound, and perfectly viable in a changing world. Certainly there was illness and poverty and hunger, but those things were ever-present for most of the population then, and crofters were better able to weather the storms than were the huddled masses in the intolerable slums of the cities.

And the brave new world across the oceans? It was in fact in those days a howling wilderness in which hardship and death were everyday companions; a wilderness which had to be faced without the strong ties and solidarity which bound together Highland society. But let us leave the past and its sad memories, and continue our journey.

Further west again, for a mile or so, and you come to Clach na Criche, the Boundary Stone, marking the boundary between two old parishes. It is an odd rib of rock coming out of the low cliff by the roadside, and pierced by a window just wide enough to squeeze through. You must take a mouthful of water from the nearby burn, and hold it in your mouth as you pass through the rock eye. Then you swallow the water, and make a wish. No guarantee comes with this, but you have nothing to lose, either.

Just a mile further on are the ruins of Killundine Castle, *Casteall nan Con* or Castle of the Dog. They are not very impressive, and are only of the 16th century, but the site is a spectacular one, looking across the Sound to Aros Castle on Mull. Presumably the Dog Castle was a hunting lodge for Aros.

There is a most impressive cairn a little beyond the castle, just by a mile stone. It lies to the right of the road. It is about 250 feet in diameter, but seems never to have been excavated. It is called Cairn na Cailleach, the Cairn of the Old Woman, and there is a very fragmentary and confusing legend about it, concerning an old woman who tried to build a bridge across the Sound of Mull.

Close by are two very impressive stone circles. From the number of these circles, cairns and incised stones, one must conclude that there was a considerable and highly developed population hereabout in prehistoric days, and that Columba must have had quite a task in his proseletysing, for there is no reason to suppose that the Christianity brought by Columba was particularly welcome.

The metalled road ends just three miles further on, at Bunavoullin, in the Drimnin district. From there on, there are no public roads in the whole vast area. However, a very passable foot track continues from Bunavoullin to Drimnin House and beyond, if there has not been too much recent rain, right round Auliston Point, where Loch Sunart joins the Sound of Mull, and then through empty hills to Loch na Droma Buidhe and Isle Oronsay. That really is the end.

If you can, though, travel through those hills, and experience the total quietness of them. If you get to Oronsay and Loch na Droma Buidhe you may well find yourself surrounded by seals, for they breed here.

Be careful about Isle Oronsay. The name always means a half-tide island, and at low spring tides you can cross dry shod to the island. But you may not get back dry shod, for the tide comes in quickly.

You have come so far, and now you must go back the same way. Back down the Sound, through Loch Aline, on to the main (!) road. This time though, stop and look at the quite remarkable architecture of the village school at Claggan, and try to think why it should ever have been built like that. On further, to where the main road swings left, and the B8043 will lead you through Kingairloch and back to Inversanda on the road to Corran Ferry and Fort William.

This is new country, and although it may not be the most direct road, it is supremely well worth taking. To begin with, as in Morvern, there is only one road in the whole of the Kingairloch area, and that one road leaves the whole vast southern portion quite untouched. There are a few tracks into that wilderness, and they are very much worth taking. On foot, of course. They will take you over hills and through glens seamed with lovely burns and patched with lochans, past a hundred deserted crofts and finally, most of them, to the shores of Loch Linnhe, with a host of lonely beaches, and Lismore, the verdant island, close across the water.

There is something strange about the place-names here. For example, 'Kingairloch' means The Head of Loch Gair, but there is no Loch Gair. There is also a Loch a Choire, but a corrie is a rocky valley you find high in the hills, certainly not at sea level.

Indeed, there is also something strange about the history of this area. In the bay of Camus Chil Malieu is the settlement of Cilmalieu, and this remote hamlet was once the centre of Kilmallie parish, the whole 444 square miles of it, the biggest in Scotland, which included the large settlement of Fort William and even Ben Nevis. Yet there is not the slightest trace now of any important religious settlement at Kilmallie.

As you leave the A884 and travel along the high B8043 there are some magnificent views of mountains, and especially of Beinn Mheadoin. It isn't much of a mountain really, but it certainly has regal pretensions. Later, Mheadoin is rather overshadowed by the higher hills of Faer Bheinn and Bein na Cille and especially by Beinn Mhead Loin. None of them reach the Munro mark of 3,000 feet, but they are all fine hills, rising steeply from the sea.

The road continues past Loch Uisge, long and narrow with some sandy beaches where many deer come to drink, but now, like so much else, despoiled by fish farm cages. After rising and falling for some miles, the road drops down to the tiny hamlet of Kingairloch. Nothing much there, if you discount wonderful panoramas of the Firth of Lorne, Lismore, Loch Linnhe and distant mountains dreaming in sunlight. The hamlet lies at the head of the deep bay of Camus na Croise and again the name indicates an early and important Christian settlement.

The Galmadale river enters the sea here, running down Glen Galmadale from the cliffs and peaks of Fuar Bheinn. It is a pretty place indeed. Pity that a supremely ugly 'Telecommunication Centre' has been erected recently just by the road. It is as incongruous as a boil would be on the neck of the Mona Lisa.

From Kingairloch the road passes by the shore, squeezed by impressive cliffs and haunted by many wild goats. It then turns inland, through country gradually becoming more fertile and cultivated, to Inversanda, where it rejoins the A861 for Corran Ferry and Fort William.

DETAIL FROM INVERURIE STONE

CORMORANT

STRONTIAN, ACHARACLE AND MOIDART

This is the only circular tour possible in this whole area. It has been made possible only in the last few years, when a truly magnificent new road has been cut through the splendours of Moidart, from Kinlochmoidart to Loch Ailort. This road traverses some of the finest scenery in the whole of Scotland. It is quite a wide and fast road, if you are foolish enough to use it so. If you do, you will miss some great joys.

Starting again from Fort Willliam and crossing Corran Ferry, travel to Strontian by A861, just as on the Morvern tour.

Strontian is a rather strange little village to find in north-west Scotland. Apart from its Highland setting of hills and loch, it is very reminiscent of an English village, with its green surrounded by great trees. Highland villages generally do not have a centre as English villages do: they developed in a different way.

Most of the present day Highland communities are in fact relics of the Clearances, when the small farmers cleared from the ancient centralised villages in the hills were dumped down on useless ground near the shore, and there built new cottages (hovels, rather)

wherever they found a suitable piece of ground. There was no centre to these new communities, no village greens, just cottages spread over the more-or-less level land, where new fields had to be cleared, and indeed new soil made, with seaweed and infinite back-breaking labour.

Strontian did not develop in that way, for much of its history has been dictated by English enterprise. After 1745, the notorious York Buildings Company acquired this area, describing at it the time as "a filthy clachan". They worked lead in the hills above the village, and the workings are still plain and interesting to see. The mineral strontium was also first discovered there in 1787, and took its name from the village. Strangely, in view of its later uses, strontium was not of very much value, being used chiefly for giving crimson flames in fireworks. Later, it was found that it could be used in purifying sugar, but there was not much call for that, either, and mining ceased in 1871.

However, those volcanic hills above the village contain a very peculiar cocktail of minerals, and periodically there are new proposals for mining them. Most recently, the aim was to mine mud for use in oil wells, or so it was said.

Today, Strontian is the place chosen by the Highlands and

Islands Development Board for an experiment in breathing new life into moribund Highland villages. This has entailed building a whole complex of information centre, shops, restaurant, houses, etc. It is a noble effort, and really very well done, blending unobtrusively into the landscape.

Although perhaps there is not much to detain you in Strontian -- apart from excellent hotels -- time spent in the area is very much worthwhile. To begin, Strontian lies at the head of Loch Sunart, twenty miles long and magnificent beyond parallel. Look down the Loch from Strontian, and there is a sight which epitomises all the beauty, romance and sadness of the Highlands. Of course, should it be raining (and rain is not unknown) you will see nothing, but just wait a while. The rain will pass and glory will re-appear in a resurrection of beauty, clean washed and gleaming.

As you leave the village and cross the bridge, a minor road turns sharply right, running up the river. Take that road and travel up the glen, through Scotstown (as distinct, no doubt, from Englishtown in the old days). There are a lot of little houses up there, many of them restored and attractive. It is a fine little glen, and at the head of it there is a parking and picnic site where you can leave your car and walk along a grand Nature Trail through a Nature Reserve.

It seems odd that such a thing should be necessary in the remote Highlands. It is very interesting, though, with fine panoramas of distant hills. The trail ends at the old lead mines, and you will surely wonder at the sheer doggedness and persistence of the men who produced those great spoil hills, walls and galleries using only their own muscles and hand tools.

You can drive further along the road, although it is steep, narrow and twisting. In two miles it climbs to 1121 feet, and then drops sharply downwards. From the summit there is a wholly enchanting view of Loch Doilet, set in trees and framed by blue mountains. The road drops down to the Loch. If you continue (and the latter part you must walk) you can reach the shore of Loch Shiel, walking down the bank of the short, broad Polloch River. It is all very beautiful indeed, and certainly not too strenuous.

There are other walks in this district, and some of them certainly are strenuous, taking you through wild and remote country. Even in the best of weather they should never be tackled without proper clothing and preparation. A forest track runs five miles from the head of Loch Doilet to the lonely house of Resaurie. Now there is a place to get away from it all!

Two tracks run from Resaurie all the way back to Ardgour, through some of the hardest but loveliest scenery in all of Scotland. They go by Mam Beathaig, Bealach Garbh and Sgridain passes, with steep climbs and, even steeper drops, to Inverscaddle on Loch Linnhe. Do not think to do either walk except on a long day, but do them if you can: the effort is repaid a thousandfold.

Back, then, to the main road at Strontian. All the way from Strontian to Kinlochmoidart this main road is single track, with passing places. It has been greatly 'improved' in recent years, with many sharp bends and blind summits removed, but care is still necessary. And please, if you are just dandering on, enjoying the lovely scenery, do let other people overtake you. Go off the road into a passing place. Not everyone on the road is a tourist.

There used to be a floating church moored off-shore just by Strontian. In 1843 the people of the area were refused permission to erect their own church, and they refused to attend the established church. This was after the Disruption, when the Free Church split away. Apart from the theological arguments involved in the Disruption, there were very practical economic and political issues. Ministers of the Established Church were appointed by the landowners, and only too often they counselled the congregation to accept in all humility the policy of clearing people off the land so that sheep could be accommodated, to the greater profit of the landowners.

This was the case in Strontian, and Sir James Riddell, who had recently purchased Ardnamurchan, refused even to permit the building of a Free Church. So the congregation raised the enormous sum of £1400 and acquired a floating church. The good Sir James must have been livid at having his wishes circumvented in that way, and one can well imagine his teeth-gnashing and moustache-pulling. Still, the floating church was bought, and towed to Strontian and moored off-shore. It was noticed that for every hundred worshippers, the hulk sank one inch into the water, and it was said that the popularity of every preacher could be judged to the inch!

There is another grand track for walking up into the hills about a mile out of Strontian. Turn right off the road at the Ben View Hotel, and start walking. Go far enough, and you reach Loch Doilet and Loch Shiel. It is not such a rough or strenuous outing as the walk from Doilet to Ardgour, but it, too, is very fine. It takes you past more of the old lead mines which riddle these hills, and eventually right through to Loch Doilet.

The road from Strontian to Salen runs mostly along the shore of the Loch, through woods with fine views of Morvern across the Loch and of the Sunart Hills, especially Ben Resipol, to the right.

Ben Resipole is very much worth walking up. Well, more of a

scramble, really. There is a clear enough track from behind the house at Resipole Farm and you will find that easily enough, because the only caravan site in the district is there, right by the edge of the Loch. For Ben Resipole, follow the stream uphill.

When you get to the top (and it is 2750 feet, straight up from sea level), you will be rewarded with views of a truly glorious Highland tapestry. Distant lochs gleam like pewter amongst hills sweeping and swelling in beauty. Islands lift like dreams from far seas. And it is quiet, with just a breeze soughing through the thin herbage, and bringing faint scents of salt and smoke and damp earth. Altogether lovely.

As you continue along the road, you will find that Salen is hardly even a village -- a shop, an hotel, a Post Office and a scatter of houses. It has a grand position, though, and the view from the top of the hill above the village is very fine.

Today, instead of going down the hill to the Ardnamurchan wonderland, keep straight on the A861 to Acharacle.

Before going further, let us settle the question of how to pronounce Acharacle. It is 'A-har-ackle'. Pronounce it 'Ack-a-rackle', and there will be some hidden smiles. By some Gaelic semantic alchemy, the name is derived from Ath-Thorceill or Torquil's Ford. Torquil was one of those bloody-minded Danes of the old days, who came ashore to plunder Moidart. He began his pillage near Dorlin, and close by there is a Lochan na Falla, the Loch of Blood to commemorate it all. His ford can still be seen crossing the River Shiel just by Acharacle.

Acharacle itself is a rather scattered and shapeless village, much more typical of Highland communities than the rather 'Englishised' Strontian. It lies on level land at the foot of Loch Shiel. Its main attraction is the view of distant hills, although for anglers the short River Shiel is world-famous for its salmon and sea trout.

Just through the village, instead of continuing on the main road to Kinlochmoidart, take the B8044 to Kentra and Ardtoe. At first it is perhaps not a very inspiring road, mostly going over rather

ACHARACLE

featureless peat moss. But there are not so many places now where peat is still cut for fires: this is one of them and the sight is interesting.

You will almost certainly see piles of peats cut to the size and shape of bricks, stacked up to dry. Cutting the blocks from the peat-face is not too difficult, for when it is wet the peat is soft and buttery. However, the task of cutting, drying and carrying enough peats for the winter months is very considerable. Not many crofters tackle it these days, chiefly perhaps because most crofters are elderly; the young and strong must leave for places where there is at least the possibility of employment.

Contrary to what many people think, peat is not a sort of half-made, immature coal. It is the remains of bog plants and heather, sealed from the air for many centuries and preserved remarkably well. Peat is also itself a remarkable preservative. Tree trunks, animal bodies and even human bodies have been found in peat bogs, perfectly preserved and just as recognisable as on the day they died, many centuries earlier.

In Ireland, the great peat bogs are mined and exploited: in Scotland, generally, they are ignored. In Ireland, the national Bord Na Mona excavates peat in vast quantities, for use in electric generating stations, railway engines and factory boilers. Most domestic fuel there is peat, compressed into hard shiny blocks, and sold in every corner shop. After the peat is removed, the land is restored to excellent pasture. Here in Scotland little is done with this energy source, and the little grows less.

Leaving the peat moss, you approach the coast, and the road takes you through some delightful wooded straths and then down to the lovely Ardtoe. This is an area of tiny beaches, rock and rock ribs and little coves. All a great joy. There is a Government-sponsored experimental fish station at Ardtoe. It doesn't look like much (except a bit of an eyesore), but it is a major employer in this very remote area, and some of the experiments made here in sea fish breeding and rearing may well allow us to feed when the seas are finally emptied of their natural harvests.

As usual, you must go back the way you came, to Acharacle and the main road. This time, turn left on to the main road, cross the very shapely bridge over the River Shiel and continue a few hundred yards to where the main road turns right for Kinlochmoidart. Go straight ahead, though, for Castle Tioram.

The road to the castle passes along the River Shiel, and you can see the fishing stances erected there for anglers. Don't be tempted to drop a line in the water, though. It is all very private. Even 700 years ago the great monk Adamnan was impressed by the quality and quantity of the salmon taken out of the River Shiel.

This is a fine little road running through quite magnificent old trees, then over a strange wasteland, before dropping down to the delightful Castle Tioram. Unless you have been unlucky enough to get there at high water spring tides, you can walk dry shod to the castle, which stands on a rock a hundred or so yards from the shore.

It is a fine, very romantic ruin, roofless now and for the last two hundred years. Amy, divorced wife of John, Lord of the Isles, had the castle built in the mid-14th century. Her son by John was called Ranald, and he was the founder of the vast and powerful Clanranald, which was based on Castle Tioram.

There are many legends and stories about Castle Tioram, and some of them might be true. In the mid-16th century, the clan chief was John of Moidart. He was chief by popular acclaim, not by right of birth. Such democratic doings were indeed possible in the clan

CASTLE TIORAM

system. However, it happened that John had gone off to war, and was captured and imprisoned in the south. A clan without a chief was like a chicken without a head -- quite useless, easy meat for any marauder, and liable to go off in any direction. So the elders invited Ranald Fraser, who was their chief by birth, to visit Castle Tioram and take his place as chief. Naturally, being the Highlands, a great feast was prepared to welcome him, but Ranald (perhaps he had been living in Aberdeen!) enquired how much this feast was costing, and complained at the waste. Very justifiably, he was promptly chased away, to the indignation of the Frasers.

Out of that piece of silliness, a whole battle ensued, The Battle of the Shirts, fought between the Frasers and the men of Clanranald on one hot July day, when the warriors stripped off their shirts, the better to lay about them. Much of Highland clan history is just as bloody and childish as that one incident.

The Frasers, incidentally, were soundly beaten in the Battle of the Shirts, and John, released from his imprisonment, ruled his clan for long years afterwards.

It was also in John's time that some money was stolen from the Castle. Two men and a girl were accused of the theft. The men were hanged from the gallows tree, but the girl was tied to a rock in the bay, and drowned as the tide came in, with John standing close by to hear any posible last confession. There was none, and the girl was drowned on the rock still known as Sgear Nighean Sheamais -- The Rock of James's Daughter. Strangely enough, a good horde of silver Elizabethan coins was found last century in the woods opposite the Castle. They might well have been the stolen coins for which three people died.

Donald Gorm was clan chief some time after John. He suffered, very properly, from a bad conscience, which manifested itself as a big black frog which followed him everywhere. Once, he managed to lock the frog in a dungeon before setting sail for Arisaig. A great wind blew up, and waves threatened to swamp his galley. The frog was there, floating on the water. The crew begged Donald to take it in the boat, and eventually he agreed, whereupon the gale dropped and they beached safely.

Cromwell's men occupied the castle during the Civil War, and a small cairn marks the grave of one of his men, buried alive as a punishment, although we do not know his crime.

The last of the Clanranalds to live in Tioram was Alan. He went to join the Jacobite rising in 1715, under the Earl of Mar. Doubting Mar's ability (and he was right about that), he feared that he would never return to Tioram. He ordered that the castle be burned as soon as he had left it, rather than have it occupied by others. There is a big stone on the saddle between the hills east of the castle, and Alan sat there and watched his castle burn. The stone is still called the Seat of Clanranald's Chief.

One can well understand Alan's distress, for Tioram's position is quite superb. It looks across a narrow arm of the loch to the lovely island of Shona, rich and well wooded. Out to the west the Hebrides rise in glory from the sea. Everywhere is beauty.

Everywhere, that is, but on the shore by the castle, where the desolation of the once majestic Dorlin House fouls what should be magical.

There are two good footpaths from Dorlin. The first goes straight on from where the road ends, and stays close by the shore round the headland to the deserted croft houses of Port a Bhata. It is a good walk, with lots of rocky scrambles and rock pools to explore.

The other path leads straight up the steep wooded hill opposite the Castle and behind Dorlin House. That is the track Alan took when he left his castle for the last time. At the top of the ridge, the track divides, the left fork leading to Port a Bhata, and the right across country to Blain, where the Dorlin road left the main road.

If you walk that track (and really, everyone should) you will find not only views of rare delight, but you will also discover that the light on those hills is of a strange quality and a most peculiar intensity. Perhaps it has something to do with the great open sea being so close. Whatever it is, it is rare and lovely.

By car, you must return to Blain and turn left for Kinlochmoidart. The road runs over a great peat moss to Langal. It was here that the army of the great Somerled met and defeated the Viking forces of Torquil -- he of the ford. Somerled, in fact if not at first in name, was the first Lord of the Isles. It was he who drove the invading Norwegians out of most of Western Scotland and the isles. King David I confirmed Somerled's Lordship of the Isles in 1135.

As you climb up through wooded hills, a minor road on the right leads down to Dalilea, on the shore of Loch Sheil. Beyond the farm at the end of that minor road is a foot track to a jetty. The Loch, never more than a mile or so wide, here narrows to little more than a hundred yards, and is almost completely blocked by St. Finnan's Island, Eillean Fhinnain. This is a very holy place indeed, where St. Finnan, a disciple of Columba, had his chapel. The ruins are still there, and a hand-bell rests on the altar. St. Finnan himself brought the bell from Ireland, and left a curse on anyone who dares remove it. And the curse has worked at least twice in recent years.

The island was the graveyard for the chiefs of Clanranald, and many stones lie under the long grass. Interestingly, the Catholics were always buried to the north and the Protestants to the south of the island. It is a fine and peaceful place for resting, either for an hour or for all eternity.

It was at Dalilea that the famous Gaelic poet Alexander MacDonald was brought up. His father was the Episcopalian Minister for Ardnamurchan, and each Sunday and every Sunday, he walked thirty miles over the hills to his church at Kilchoan, and thirty miles back.

DALILEA

It was also at Dalilea that Prince Charles Edward embarked on that day in August 1745, and was rowed up the Loch by twelve men of Moidart to the fateful gathering at Glenfinnan. He had walked the hills from Glen Uig, and he was to walk them again a year later, hounded by those who hunted him.

In that August of 1745, he had spent the previous night at Kinlochmoidart House, and tradition says that he walked for hours up and down a path by the house, alone and pondering. The path is still there, and still known as The Prince's Walk. Today it is rather gloomy with rhododendrons, but they can't have been there on that evening, for they were introduced into Scotland only in 1763. There are big old trees, though, and a spring of fresh water, and it must have been a soothing place to spend the last hours before embarking on such a venture as that of the '45.

Kinlochmoidart House of today is not the one where Prince

GREY SEAL AT DORLIN

KINLOCHMOIDART

Charles Edward stayed. That one was burned down in the savagery of 1746, and the little white house now standing behind the mansion was built on the site of the old house. The old lady, mother of Donald of Kinloch, the chief of his clan, was carried out of the house before it was set on fire, and she died there, under the yew trees. Donald was captured and beheaded, and his head stuck on a spike above the gate of Carlisle Castle. Donald's wife and small children fled up the glen during that night of horror, up towards Glenforslan, and a little while later she went out of her mind.

There is a grand track leading over the hills behind Dalilea Farm, all the way back to Glen Moidart. You might perhaps arrange to have someone drive your car from Dalilea to Glen Moidart, and meet there after you walk the hills. The track runs first to Brunery, and passes Torr a Bhreitheimh. This is a mound covered with loose stones and surrounded by a low stone wall. In the old days it was the place where clan chiefs dispensed their own form of no doubt rough justice. Beyond that Place of Justice, another cairn has been erected to General Ross, one-time landowner of all this countryside.

The quickest way back to the main road is by following the track to the left just past the General's Cairn, but if you keep right, you will come eventually to Glenmoidart House. Go straight on again, keeping the river to your right. This is a delightful walk, not too steep, but deep into the hills, and with a laughing river keeping you company. At Glenforslan is a waterfall that can be very impressive in a spate.

Way up the river, towards its source, are the ruined croft houses of Ulgary. Long ago a fine and famous piper lived there, and he was once visited, late at night and deep in those lonely hills, by a faery who suggested that magic powers would be given to his pipes if the piper made an extra hole in the chanter. If he did that, his pipes would ensure victory in battle whenever they were played. Very naturally, the piper followed this suggestion, and it was he and his

enchanted pipes who led the men of Glenmoidart to victory in many a battle.

The piper would not find many men to follow him today out of these so lovely but desolate glens. The Children of the Mist have vanished.

Back to the main road, which passes several cairns, commemorating places where corteges rested on their way to St. Finnan's Isle. Suddenly, as the narrow road drops through the trees to the magnificent sweep round the head of Loch Moidart, there is a most splendid panorama of hill and loch.

Down to the left of the road, in the field by the shore, is a row of beech trees. It is said that they were planted to commemorate the seven men of Moidart who first marched with Prince Charles Edward. One is a rather miserable specimen, and it is believed to have been planted by the one traitor to the cause. His tree died, and replacements have never flourished. Recently a memorial plaque has been tastefully erected on the roadside, and there you can read the story, or one version of it.

The new road to Loch Ailort begins at Kinlochmoidart, and a fine road it is. However, it was not built without destroying a lovely and unique thing, the ancient Highland road. It really was a delight, running through natural woods, narrow, rocky and steep, impossible for wheels, but ideal for feet. Well, it is gone now, and visitors can speed along in style.

At first the new road runs for a mile or two along the shore of Loch Moidart, with the faery island of Shona Beg just across the narrow channel. The tide goes far out here, and at low water you can actually reach the island by stepping stones. Shona is almost two islands, Eillean Shona and Shona Beg, the two being joined only by a very narrow neck of land. The name probably comes from Shoney, a Celtic sea god. Sacrifices, usually of fish, have been made to Shoney by fisherfolk down the ages, and even as late as the 19th century.

The island is quite delightful, richly wooded and fertile. One hundred and fifty years ago, a hundred families lived on Shona.

There was a school and a sawmill until very recently. There is a roughish track right round the whole island and some quite extraordinary views of the Hebrides, Ardtoe, Castle Tioram, Loch Moidart and the inaccessible lands across the channel. Many of the trees on the island are exotics, and were planted by Capt. Swinburne, who once owned the island and brought seeds from all over the world on his many voyages. That they have grown and flourished so well says much for the climate of North-west Scotland!

Soon, the road turns inland for a steep climb before dropping down to Glenuig. Just about where the road leaves the shore is An Dun -- The Fort. This is a dome of rock where an early Queen of Moidart is said to have built a castle. She launched an attack on the island of Eigg from An Dun, and all the monks there were slaughtered. The work of the Christian missionaries and monks was not always welcome -- it was disruptive of good order and harmony in a social order that must have seemed as though it had gone on for ever, and would ever continue.

It was at An Dun that all the treasures of the MacDonalds of Kinlochmoidart were buried for safety in 1746. Some traitor betrayed this to the Redcoats and the silver was dug up and taken away. Perhaps, though, it was not all taken. Once every seven years, it is said, a fissure opens in this rock dome, revealing great heaps of gold and silver for anyone who cares to take it. But you have only one chance: take what you can carry in your hands, for if you even turn round to pick up a basket or a bag, the fissure closes for another

SMIRISARY

seven years.

The road drops down from the summit to the little village of Glenuig. It is hard to realise today that only a very few years ago this village had never seen a motor vehicle. It was approached only from the sea or over a rough foot track from Kinlochmoidart, or from the other direction, an equally rough track from Loch Ailort.

Roughish roads run from Glenuig to Samalaman and Smirisary. Samalaman House (the name means "Summer Lands") was built as a seminary in 1783 by Bishop Alexander MacDonald. The object was to train "Heather Priests" who could speak and preach in Gaelic, and who were not the rejected youngest sons of impoverished English gentlemen, appointed to their churches by the new generation of English landowners. The seminary lasted at Samalaman until 1804, when it was transferred to the island of Lismore.

There are some strange and well-authenticated ghost stories about Samalaman. There is the black dog which passes through closed doors. There is the lady dressed in grey, who walks the corridors. And there was the time, not so long ago and still spoken of, when the house suffered badly from a freak thunder storm. It was struck repeatedly by lightning, the roof demolished and the corridors filled with fallen slates and beams. Everyone in the house and from round about rushed to help, and the laird of the day rose from his bed, dressed carefully, complete with tie and shoes, and went to help -- but he had forgotten to put on his trousers!

At the back of the big house there is a little stone shed built across a stream. This was the privy, running water and all.

There is a grand hill walk starting between Samalaman and Smirisari. This leads up to Loch ne Bairnis, and there are superb views of the Hebrides from there, of Rhum, Eigg and Muck, and even of Barra. And of course the whole great ranges of hills everywhere. Not to be missed.

Although so small and isolated, Glenuig is not without its history. It has even contributed to Scotland's culture, for it was here that the famous dance "The Eight Men of Moidart" was first performed. The tradition is that when the men of Glenuig learned that Prince Charles Edward was to land there, they promptly set to and devised this dance, which they were to perform in his honour. There were only four of them, though, for the women were off to the peats. So spades were stuck in the grass to represent their partners, and the dance was worked out, to the music of a MacDonald piper.

But the village suffered for its loyalty, or for its treason, if you look at it another way. Redcoats, under the command of a Campbell of course, came in 1748, searching for arms, and they burned the village and drove off the cattle.

From Glenuig the road continues, a ribbon of grandeur, along the shore of Loch Ailort, bright, colourful and framed dramatically by the Morar Hills. There are islands off shore, and they seem to float in a sea which often is almost impossibly blue.

One of the islands is Eillean Nan Gobha -- Goat Island. This was a very ancient stronghold, and there are two vitrified forts on its peak, one with walls six feet thick and 120 yards around. Although impossible to date precisely, they were probably built around 700 B.C.

Around the time of the '45, during the undeclared war between England and France, two of their frigates fought a battle in Loch Ailort. They dodged round the islands, escaping as best they could the many shallows. On shore, people watched the battle intently, for the French were allies of Prince Charles Edward (not that they gave him much help), and the English were enemies. One old man finally dropped to his knees and prayed. The others, suspicious, asked for whom he was praying. He replied that he was praying for his goats, pasturing on Goat Island, which had just come into the line of fire!

The modern road manages to skirt Bealach Breac, the Speckled Pass, which was a considerable hill to be climbed in the not-so-far-off days when only a foot track joined Loch Ailort and these lonely hamlets. There is some considerable fish farming now in the loch, and the great floats offshore each contain some thousands of salmon growing to maturity.

Inverailort House dates back to 1750, but has been much changed since then. It was also much changed by Commandos during the war. These hills and lochs were all training areas then, and the hillsides are still strewn with cartridge cases.

Just where the River Ailort runs into the Loch is a little island covered in reeds. This is an old burial ground, and when you stand on it, you have the overwhelming impression that the island is about to be swamped by the Loch. But it never is, and it is said that however deep the graves used to be dug, they always remained dry.

You join the main Mallaig-Fort William road at Loch Ailort village. Turn right for Fort William on the road described in the first tour.

This has been a long day, and however closely you looked, you cannot possibly have absorbed even a tithe of the beauties and wonders of these roads. Be wise: repeat the trip, but this time do it in the reverse direction. You will be astonished at how different everything looks.

ARDNAMURCHAN

It would be quite impossible to determine which of the tours described in this book is the most attractive. However, this tour, right down to the very tip of Ardnamurchan Point, must certainly be a candidate for being the loveliest and most interesting road in all of Scotland.

Starting from Fort William, you have the choice of again crossing Corran Ferry and runnning through Glen Tarbert to Strontian and Salen, or, better, of going round the head of Loch Eil.

The Loch Eil road is the same as that travelled on the tour to Mallaig. Take the A82 (Inverness) road out of Fort William, and turn left on to the A830 after a mile or so. Travel that road, along the north side of Loch Eil, to the head of the Loch, where the A861 turns off to the left. Take that road, running back along the opposite shore -- the southern side of Loch Eil. The road bends right to run down Loch Linnhe opposite Fort William. It is a long 45 miles by road, but only half a mile by water.

When running round Loch Eil you have to be content with distant views of blue and sparkling mountains, and very fine views they are. But running down the western side of Loch Linnhe, the great mountains tower above you, and the glens invite you to walk them.

Glen Gour runs down to the sea at Clovalin and Salachan Bay. The glen gives you a magnificent five mile tramp into the hills, culminating at Loch nam Gabhour. It is fine and lonely walking, through harsh rock scenery and under great cliffs.

Conaglen House is at Inverscaddle Bay, about 4 miles north of Ardgour. The house itself is if no great interest, being typical and fairly recent Scottish Baronial. The estate, though, is enormous, covering 47,000 acres. It originally belonged to the MacLeans of Ardgour, whose own landholding these days is much less than that. Glen Scaddle and Cona Glen converge at Inverscaddle, and both will give you some of the finest walking anywhere in Scotland.

Cona Glen is the more northerly of the two, and each is about ten miles long, running into the wild mountains between Loch Linnhe, Loch Shiel and Loch Sunart. The peaks rise up to 2520 feet. If you take the Cona Glen, there are two passes to cross, Bealach Sgriadain and Bealach Gaoith, before reaching the head of Loch Hurich. Glen Scaddle will take you over Nam Beathaig to the same spot. Both tracks climb from sea level to 1700 feet, and the descent from Nam Beatheag to Resurie House is especially spectacular. The whole is dominated by the great peak of Sgur Dhommaill, at 2914 feet. It is all indeed great walking (if you are well prepared for it). The tracks eventually come down to the road head near Loch Hurich, and you might be able to arrange to be met there. (See Tour Two)

Much of the land around Ardgour is held by the MacLean's of Ardgour, but it hasn't always been theirs. They acquired it only in the 15th century, and before that it was MacMasters' territory. Some time in the 15th century, though, Donald MacLean slew the MacMasters' chieftain, and for good measure also killed the ferryman who brought him over to Ardgour and betrayed his own chief. Donald argued, very reasonably, that if the ferryman betrayed one chief, he could well betray another, and so was better dead.

Ardgour House is attractive, even if quite modern. The present house, which is a mile and half up a wooded valley from the road, replaced the old house which burned down in 1820. It is a pleasant building, of three storeys, Georgian in style. The Forestry Commission has now taken over much of the 40,000 acres which made up the estate in the last century.

Behind the house is MacLean's Towel, a waterfall. It is said that the MacLeans will be in Ardgour until the Towel runs dry.

From Ardgour, the road runs alongside Loch Linnhe to

Inversanda, where the minor road to Kingairloch turns to the left. Like the name 'Kingairloch', the name 'Inversanda' is rather strange, since it is on the river Tarbert, at the foot of Glen Tarbert, and there is no 'Sanda' anywhere about.

The dramatic run through Glen Tarbert and down to Strontian, with the first glimpse of Loch Sunart from the head of the Glen, has already been described in Tour Two. And the road from Strontian to Salen has been covered in Tour Three. At Salen, instead of continuing on the main road (A861) to Acharacle, turn left down the hill past the hotel, on B8007.

First, though, stop on top of the hill, by the Coast Guard hut, and look down over the village and down the Loch. There is not much to the village -- one hotel, a Post Office, a shop and a scatter of houses. But the view is superb. The Loch is cradled in the great hills of Morvern and Sunart, some wooded and some awesomely bare. The Loch, which at 20 miles is one of the longest in Scotland, seems to be sealed off by the island of Carna in the distance. It is all a rare and lovely sight, and never more so than when rain squalls are

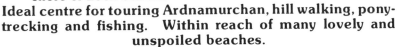

chasing over the Loch, hiding and revealing those great hills. Or perhaps on a blue and frosty winter day, when the colours are all sharp and fresh. Unforgettable.

Ardnamurchan is really a very strange and remote place. The tip of the peninsula is the furthest western point of the British mainland, indeed further west than Belfast. Although so remote, it played a pivotal role in history long past, and it has been inhabited from the dawn of time. There are remnants of the Stone Age, of the Beaker Folk and of Bronze Age man here. It appears to have been quite peaceful until the Vikings appeared in their swift galleys in the 9th century.

In 1266, the leader of the Vikings was one Muchdragon. Like so many of them, he appears to have been very randy, as well as very ferocious, and he greatly desired the wife of one of his vassals. She was a comely lass, and when Muchdragon sent word to his vassal that he was coming visiting, everyone knew what that meant. Greatly worried, the vassal and his wife understood that the one most in danger was the husband, since the wife and her chastity were safe so long as he lived. They planned that the husband would run away when Muchdragon appeared, and so that he could run more quickly than Muchdragon in all his panoply of war, he would dress only in his sark.

That is what happened, and Muchdragon, seeing the fleeing husband, unarmed except for a small battleaxe, gave chase. It was a very close thing, and at one point, half way up Beinn Hiant, Muchdragon actually grasped the man's sark and tore it. The desperate husband turned and threw his axe, and split the skull of the frustrated Viking. That happened on Beann na Urchrach, the Hill of the Throw, after they had run all the way up Clac na Coiridh, the Hollow of the Race. Not quite certain of what had happened, the desperate husband raced to the top of Beinn Hiant. Eventually he, and his still chaste wife, escaped to Islay.

Iain Sprangaich -- John the Bold -- learned what had happened, and seized his chance, now that Muchdragon was dead, by forthwith claiming possession of the whole peninsula. His tribe became known as the MacIans, and held the land for generations, under a grant made to them by King David II in 1344.

Of course, the writ of feudal kings did not amount to a great deal in those parts, just as today the laws made in London are not given much heed. The Macdonalds of Lochalsh invaded in 1515, and besieged the MacIans castle at Mingary, by Kilchoan. Still, the MacIans hung on until 1626 when the Campbells took over Ardnamurchan, as part of the seemingly endless battle between the MacDonalds and the Campbells. The MacIans were driven out, and they took to piracy, but finally were cornered and slaughtered in Loch Moidart.

That was the end of the MacIans as a separate clan: they became part of the MacDonalds, and it was the sad remnants of the MacIans who were slaughtered by the Campbells in Glencoe. Strange to think that it all took place because Muchdragon wanted to have his evil way with the bonny wife of one of his vassals.

The Campbells did not hold Ardnamurchan for long. By this time in the long history of the clans, money was beginning to be important to the Clan Chiefs, and in the early part of the 19th century Ardnamurchan was sold to the first modern proprietor. This was the rather eccentric Sir Alexander Murray. It was he who opened up the lead mines at Strontian, and he actually had plans drawn up for high level canals running from the lead mines to deep water near Fort William. He also sought to establish, of all things, a straw hat factory at Strontian, to employ the miners' wives. Not surprisingly, Sir Alexander died a bankrupt.

Later, Sir James Riddell became proprietor, and it was he who began the pernicious eviction of the peasants to make way for his sheep. Riddell sold the estate and all its inhabitants in 1855 to James Dalgliesh who continued the evictions and clearances. It was Dalgleish who built the first mansion house at Glenborrodale on the site of a much older house.

Later in the 19th century, Dalgleish sold to C.D. Rudd, who

LOCH SUNART

had been one of the builders of the British Empire. He and Cecil Rhodes each bought a quarter share in the De Beers gold mine and diamond fields, and thus became immensely rich. More than that, though, Rudd also 'persuaded' Lobengula, Chief of the Matabele and Mashona nations, to cede him exclusive mineral rights in his kingdom. This, what the history books call 'The Rudd Concession', added half a million square miles to the British Empire, and further untold wealth to Rudd. Having bought the estate, but not greatly caring for the new mansion at Glenborrodale, Rudd built himself a castle on the same site. Astonishingly, he built it in imported red sandstone, which still strikes a sour note of incongruity in that land of grey granite. Today, the castle is an hotel, and a grand one, too.

Rudd did not last very long, and the estate, from Loch Shiel to Ardnamurchan Point, passed briefly into the hands of the Clark family of Paisley of thread fame. Kenneth Mackenzie Clark, a man of immense wealth, appears to have been a virtual moron, apart from his skills in making money. His very distinguished son, later Lord Clark and every one's favourite art historian, has described how his father read virtually nothing but the adventures of Pip, Squeak and Wilfred, an excruciatingly puerile strip cartoon in one of the daily papers, and how his most strenuous mental exercise was in striving to complete the childrens' Cross-word puzzle in the same paper.

Lord Clark also describes a most strange, feudal pattern of life in Ardnamurchan, and this in 1928.

The Clarks did not hold the estate long, though, and it passed into the hands of Lord Trent. The Trent money came from Boots The Cash Chemists.

D.H. Lawrence wrote a poem expressing his wonder that pennies passed over a counter for bottles of liniment and aspirin could ever result in a new college being built, by old Jesse Boot, in Nottingham. But those pennies, in vast quantities, did that, and they also enabled the son to buy Ardnamurchan.

Trent had a very different approach to his possession than any of the earlier proprietors. He encouraged farming and even small landowners to some extent, and although the depopulation was not halted, certainly it was slowed down during those years when Trent owned that vast property.

Today, the enormous estate is broken up. Forestry claims more and more of it. The sheep, cause of so much misery, have almost gone, and the deer forests, which followed the sheep and caused even more misery, are going fast. It's the end of an auld sang.

From Salen, the road runs along the loch and sometimes seems in danger of going right into it. It is a single track road and care is needed. There are traces of old houses all along the shore, where families settled after being driven from the fertile hills and straths. They had to find a living as best they could on those few inhospitable acres and on the frightening sea.

The older houses along this road are all relics of the time when the whole vast estate was running. There are the houses where the yacht captains lived. There is the bakehouse, the dairy farm, the laundry, the forester's house, the home farm, the factor's house. There are houses for the water bailiffs, the ghillies and the shepherds. But there are no houses for people who did not work on the estate. No crofters or smallholders.

There are many fine old trees on this stretch of road, and glimpses of the loch and distant hills. It can be idyllic and beautiful beyond words. About five miles from Salen, the road begins to climb up the flanks of Ben Laga, and just there, down on the shore, is Dun Galan, a fortified place of the old days.

It was probably there that the Swan of Sunart lived. She was a lovely girl, but not wealthy, and when the young chief fell in love with her, there was some consternation. She could bring neither power nor pelf: what was the use of marrying her? Bed her, of course, by all means, but do not marry her. But he could not bed her, for she was a chaste lady. (Or, to be cynical, perhaps she knew what stakes she was playing for, for chastity was not a particular virtue of those days.) It was marry, or nothing, so marriage it was to be.

But the young chief's mother would have none of this. She

called for a sorcerer, and he put a spell on the stubborn young woman and changed her into a swan. The young man, of course, knew nothing of this, and thought that his love had deserted him. He was sick of his passion, and languished for weeks and months along the side of the Loch, wasting his days in hunting, when he might have been profitably busy harrying his neighbours.

One day, languidly hunting, he shot an arrow at a swan which he had noticed on the shore for several days. He killed it, of course, and as it died a fluttering death, it changed again into the young chief's love. So he drew his dirk and drove it into his own heart, and died in her dead arms.

Swan Lake, move over: The Swan of Sunart came first, by a thousand years.

As you breast the rise and drop down again, you will surely notice the great square cages floating offshore by Laga Farm. There are thousands of young salmon in those cages, carefully bred and fed for the market -- if they survive long enough in those noisome fishy concentration camps ever to reach market. The conditions in which those fish are reared are strictly comparable to the rearing of battery chickens -- just as inhumane, and with an end result just as tasteless and questionable.

That is fish farming, which is spreading into every loch and inlet up the north-west coast of Scotland. Indeed, it is even spreading now to the most remote fresh-water lochs high in the hills, where there are cages used for rearing the young fish before their transfer to the cages in the sea lochs. If you have ever wondered why salmon is now so comparatively cheap and plentiful, here is the answer. But the price you pay in the supermarket for your salmon steaks in no way reflects the real price of the sea-bed pollution or the visual pollution of the landscape. That is an account which will have to be settled one day, though.

From Laga, you have a clear view of Carna, a steep and rocky island which almost bottles up both Loch Sunart and Loch Teacuis. For much of the time it is uninhabited, although there is a sheep flock there, and a few holiday houses. It wasn't always so: there used to be a goodly community on Carna, and not so long ago. There used to be seven well-known fiddlers on the island and the people were locally famous for their dancing.

Carna is closer to Morvern than to Ardnamurchan, and in those days, in the middle of last century, there was a considerable community at Rahoy, in Morvern, opposite Carna. It is recorded that one summer evening the doctor from Rahoy was swimming over to Carna, bound for a bit of courting, when he met the island bull, swimming to the mainland. It is said that in mid-channel he raised his top hat to the bull and said: "Same business as myself, I'll be bound." And lest you think it just a story, the doctor was John MacLachlan and the bull was Fergus, and both are still spoken of as though it all happened yesterday.

Glenborrodale, two miles from Laga, is hardly a village -- just what was the estate factor's house, the home farm, the saw mill and the castle itself. Looking out over Glenborrodale Bay, though, there is a wonderful vista of hills and water. As befits the vicinity of the castle, there are fine trees and rhododendrons here, and the castle grounds -- now the hotel grounds -- are filled with masses of very colourful bushes and shrubs. It is very attractive.

The little island offshore is Risga. It seems that for many long years Risga was a holy place, for there are many engraved rocks there, with the ancient, perhaps Druidical, cup-and-ring marks. Stone kists, which might be coffins, have also been found.

Just by the castle a rough road goes up the hill to what used to be the estate dog kennels. Occasionally carriage lights are seen on this road, and ghostly hoof beats heard. When that happens, death is approaching.

The name 'Borrodale' is said to be derived from *Borrodil,* a Norse warrior who was killed there, and buried hard by Casteall Breac -- The Speckled Castle -- on the hill behind the farm. Nothing remains of that old Norse watchtower today except a heap of rough stones, but if you stand by them, you get a lovely view of Sunart and the Sound of Mull.

It is easy enough to imagine how those warriors of old kept watch from there, waiting perhaps for easy prey for their swift galley beached in the bay below. Or perhaps ready to defend their land and their poor flocks and harvest if stronger foes appeared, sweeping down The Swan's Path from distant Norway.

There are some good tracks in the hills from Glen Borrodale. One leads all the way to Acharacle (keep right where the track divides), past lonely Loch Laga. It is a walk of rare delight on a spring day when the hills seem to come alive again after a winter's sleep. The left hand track leads to little Lochan nan Fiann and ends there. This hinterland of Ben Laga holds many such lochans, and they are very quiet and secret places.

Another track (keeping left at Glenborrodale) leads across high and wild country all the way to Ockle on the north coast. Now that is a great walk! It passes over quite high country, with views of the islands in all their majesty. It passes several most attractive lochans, and finally follows the little Ockle Burn through a wooded valley to the sea. Ockle is the end of the road, and the end of this tour, and it might be possible to arrange that the walkers take this lovely track, while someone drives all the way round to meet them at Ockle. And don't worry, you can't miss each other, for there is only one road.

Just beyond Glenborrodale castle, where the road dips down again to the sea, is a tiny rocky bay, and this is one of the few places actually on the road where you are likely to see seals. They come up onto the rocks there, and seem to be quite undisturbed by traffic -- not that there is much traffic.

The road continues, twisting and turning (although not nearly as much as it used to), to Glenmore, where it passes round the head of a bay brilliant with saffron weed at low water. The road then climbs steeply through trees to Ardslignish.

At the top of the brae there is a most wonderful view back up Loch Sunart to Beinn Resipol. Across the Loch is the island of Oronsay, with lonely Loch na Droma Buidhe behind. There is Loch

CAMUS NAN GHEALL

Teacuis running deep into Morvern's blue hills. Down the Loch is the Sound of Mull and Mull itself. Often the colours are of an almost unbelievable brilliance, and every fold of those great hills, and every peak, reflects in water so still it might be painted. The view from Ardslignish, on a clear day, is one of the great sights of this world.

In a field at the top of the brae is St. Columba's Well. It appears that once, when proseletysing in Ardnamurchan, the saint met a couple of his converts, who were sorely troubled because their child had not been baptised. There was no water there then, for the saint to make holy and perform the ceremony of baptism, so he knelt and prayed, and miraculously water sprang from the ground where he knelt, and has continued springing ever since.

From Ardslignish, the road continues, very dramatically, high above the lovely Camus nan Geall, which might mean The Bay of the Small Boats, or perhaps the Bay of the Strangers. It would be very strange indeed if you can pass this without walking down to that little stretch of fertile land and welcoming sand.

There is a tiny burial ground there, Cladh Chiarian -- Graveyard of Ciaran. St. Ciaran, of the ancient Celtic Church, and beloved of Columba, died in Ireland on 9th September, 548, and Columba arranged for his body to be brought here for burial.

At the south-west corner of the stone-walled burial ground is a very ancient standing stone with interesting carving. There is an animal which might be a dog, and two crosses. This could be the stone of St. Ciaran. This burial ground is the only piece of land in Ardnamurchan which still belongs to the Campbells, and it contains some of their ancient chiefs.

As you walk round the bay, keep your eyes open, for semi-precious stones are washed down here from the hills. Amethyst, cairngorm and sapphire are all found, if you know what they look like in the rough.

Walking, or rather scrambling, round the coast here is great fun. There is plenty of beachcombing for shells, sea-carved wood and strange stones. The natural rock gardens of the coast are always delightful, and you might well be rewarded with a sight of red deer herds. Go far enough round this coast, and you reach the high and interesting cliffs of McLean's Nose.

Back at Camus Nan Geall, there are some well-preserved ruins of old houses, now long deserted. They were the original houses built by peasants evicted from their holdings in the hills, and you can easily envisage the pattern of their life from the design of their houses.

After its dramatic, corniche-like path high above Camus nan Geall, the road turns inland, passing Loch Mudle and skirting Beann Hiant. Really, this Holy Mountain only reaches 1729 feet, but it rears straight up from the sea, and is fine and stately.

Alasdair Mac Maighsir Alasdair, or Alexander MacDonald, lived at the foot of Ben Hiant. He was one of the great Gaelic and Jacobite poets. Born in the early years of the 18th century, Alasdair was a son of the local Episcopalian clergyman, and was himself a school master in Ardnamurchan. He produced one of the first Gaelic-English Dictionaries, and his poems, vividly descriptive of the Highlands in the last days of the clan society, are still remembered and loved.

Alisdair was out in the '45, and fought bravely for his misguided Prince. He escaped after Culloden, and sheltered in the hills above Arisaig. Eventually, he returned to Edinburgh and taught there, but returned to his beloved West Highlands to die at Arisaig. Oddly, he took to imbibing opium, and spent some time in a madhouse.

But it was Dr. John MacLachlan (he who met the bull when swimming to Carna on some amorous occasion) who, in his poems, described and mourned the vicious clearances which left Ardnamurchan a hell for people, a haven for sheep and a heaven for the incoming proprietor. He looked at Ben Hiant in its new desolation and noted that:

> *Where the bairns and hearth fires were,*
> *There the rushes highest grow.*

Today, rank upon rank of young pine trees march up the flanks of Ben Hiant and occupy the old fertile parks like some invading fascist army. They ensure that never again will there be bairns and hearth fires where the trees now grow high.

And with the trees come changes in all the fauna and flora, and maybe (who knows?) even of climate. The deer are now fenced out of the fertile and more sheltered lowlands and must survive as best they can on the winter-blasted heights.

At the foot of Ben Hiant, a roughish road takes off to the right and leads directly to the quiet north coast of Ardnamurchan, through Kilmory, then on to Swordle and Ockle, which really is the end of the road, although not of the foot track.

The name 'Kilmory' derives from *Cille Mhoire* or the Cell of Mary, and the existing church is built over a much older one, dating back to the earliest days of Christianity in Scotland. Bodies were

GRAVEYARD, KILMORY

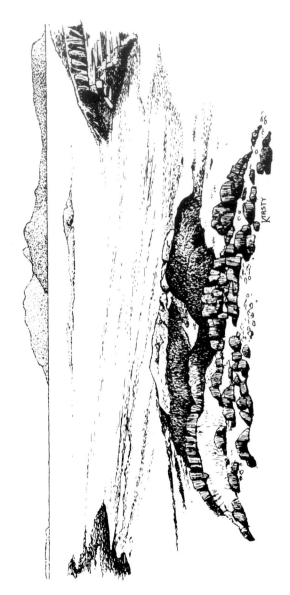

RHUM AND EIGG FROM SWORDLE

brought here for burial from far away, many of them by sea, for this was a very holy place. Within the churchyard itself is an ancient font, which is never dry of water, even during the longest drought.

This north coast, when you reach it, is great for pleasure. It is all rocky coves, pools and tiny deserted beaches, cut off from the rest of the world. There are caves, too. Scrambling and beach combing there is a fine way indeed to pass the whole of a long summer day. And the views are spectacular, with the Inner Hebrides rising lovely out of the sea.

From Ockle, a foot track continues right along the coast, finally ending in distant Acharacle. Not a Sunday afternoon stroll for the timid, perhaps, but a wonderful and very rewarding walk.

There are great caves beyond Ockle, and one of them is still known as Uaimh Chloinm Iaian, or MacIain's Cave. The MacIain clan, what was left of them, took refuge in that cave one winter's day in 1624, when the Campbells were investing Mingary Castle. They were safe enough there, in that rocky wilderness, but unfortunately it snowed that night, and in the morning a Campbell scout spotted a solitary line of footprints leading to the cave, where a straggler had joined his comrades during the night. The Campbells hastened from Mingary and lit a great fire at the mouth of the cave, and suffocated all those within.

The main road continues from the Kilmory junction down to the village of Kilchoan. Just before you enter the village, a private road to the left runs down a short distance to Mingary Castle. It leaves the main road just by Tom-a-chrochaire, The Hill of the Hangman. Rough feudal justice used to be dispensed there, with the hangman standing by ready to enforce it.

Mingary Castle is a most interesting fortalice but unfortunately it is crumbling fast, and is unsafe to enter. Surely it is already past time for some preservation work to be done there.

From its rocky promontory it dominated both the Sound of Mull and Loch Sunart, just as its close relative Castle Tioram dominated the sea routes of the Inner Hebrides.

Mingary is a castle of enceinte, that is, there is a battlemented and defensible outer wall protecting an inner keep, itself fortified. The outer walls still stand 25 feet high, with a parapet. It is hexagonal in shape, and the foundations follow the natural slopes of the rock on which it was built in the 14th century. Inside the walls, the oblong keep was probably added later. It is higher than the walls, and faces inland.

There is a ditch on the landward side, and perhaps once there was a drawbridge, but the principal entrance is from the sea, up a flight of steps cut into the cliff. And that is as it should be, for once the highway was the sea, and the purpose of this castle was to guard the sea routes, not the land routes, for they hardly existed.

This was the seat of the MacIains, and later of the Campbells in Ardnamurchan. Colkitto MacDonald, that fiery lieutenant of Montrose, captured Mingary in 1644. It was used as a prison for Covenanters, and the Campbells held it for the King during Prince Charles Edward's rising in 1745. It was also in Mingary that King James IV received the submission of the Lords of the Isles. Indeed, he received it twice, in 1493 and 1495, and neither submission held for long.

In 1515, the MacDonalds of Lochalsh arrived to besiege Mingary, but it was too strong for them, and they were driven off. In 1588, Maclean of Duart besieged it, with help from Spaniards, whose ship, one of the Armada, had put into Tobermory for repairs. Scotland, an independent kingdom in those days, was of course not involved in England's wars. Maclean, even with Spanish help, failed to take the castle, but the attempt is commemorated by the name of the bay below the castle, which is still known as Port Nan Spainteach or Spaniards Bay.

Later, in 1625, the Earl of Argyll granted the castle to the Campbells, without saying a word, apparently, to the real owners, the MacIains, who, dispossessed, took to piracy and eventually perished. So, Mingary has had a long history, much of it blood-boltered. But that's the story of the Highlands, anyway.

Kilchoan is a scattered little village on a raised beach above the sea, facing Tobermory on Mull. The name comes from *Cill Chomhghain* -- The Church of Congan. Congan, a missionary, came here from Ireland in the 7th century.

Do visit the churchyard at Kilchoan and look at the grave of the notorious tacksman Donald MacColl. He was one of those renegade Scots prepared to carry out the filthy work of clearances and evictions for the new English landowners. In this case, MacColl worked for Dalgliesh, and a fine ruthless pair they must have been.

In 1844 Dalgliesh ordered the eviction of a farmer from Ormsaigmore, by Kilchoan. This man had championed the cause of others evicted, and he was a popular figure. Dalgleish refused to renew his lease, and his tacksman MacColl tried to do the job of eviction. He was driven off in disarray. He sent to Oban for soldiers to help, but no one would man a boat to bring the soldiers over. After a while, one man was persuaded by threats to transport them, but, in fear, he brought them only as far as Maclean's Nose, down the coast. McColl was then able to carry out his eviction.

The man, six children and a bed-ridden, ill wife were thrown out of their house and watched it destroyed, and lived afterwards for six weeks on the shore, covered by an old sail. The sick wife died, but before she died she cursed McColl and all his works, saying that his soul would go to everlasting perdition, and that as a proof of that, no grass would ever grow on his grave. McColl died, and was buried in the old Kilchoan churchyard. No grass does grow on his grave, but only nettles and docks. See it for yourself.

As John MacLachlan wrote:

The blind, the aged and the imbecile,
Venting curses on thy greed.

A ship sailed from Tobermory for Australia on September 27, 1837, with 322 passengers, and 105 of them were from Ardnamurchan, the youngest and strongest and the best of the peasant farmers. Many had gone before them, and there were many to follow, until the land was empty.

It was the Campbells of Mingary who gave the first warning about the landing of Prince Charles Edward, and that he had raised his standard at Glenfinnan. The minister of Kilchoan, a Campbell of course, weedled the information out of his maidservant, and promptly reported to the officers in Mingary Castle. They sent off a messenger to Ardtornish, who sent another to Oban, who sent another to Inverary Castle, great centre of the Campbell empire, where the news was received only two days after the standard had been raised.

Cattle from the outer islands used to be landed at Kilchoan, for the long trek south to the great cattle fairs. You can still trace some of the old drove roads -- the lovely track beyond Ockle to Acharacle is one of them.

Ormsaigbeg and Ormsaigmore are just beyond Kilchoan. At Ormsaigbeg, Angus, Lord of the Isles, was murdered by an Irish harper in 1490. There are the ruins of a small 15th century castle keep here, known as the Black Castle of the Minstrels. No-one seems to know why there should have been minstrels there, or an Irish harper.

Fingal's Griddle, by Ormsaigmore, was once a group of standing stones, grey and very ancient, but is now no more than a pathetic heap. It does, though remind us again of just how long man has lived in these parts, and how each society has striven to leave permanent records behind it.

Beyond Sron Beagh, past Ormsaigmore, cliffs rear steeply out of the sea, and below those cliffs, accessible only from the sea, is a big cave hidden behind a waterfall. It was here that the Kilchoan body-snatchers lurked. They worked Kilchoan graveyard and elsewhere, and carried the bodies they snatched by sea to Oban. They had their boat painted white on one side and black on the other, to confuse any watchers. That trick they copied from the MacIains, who painted their pirate galleys in that way.

A MacBraynes ferry, now for both passengers and cars, runs daily from Kilchoan to Tobermory during the summer months, and gives visitors to Kilchoan the chance to see something of Mull, as well as an enjoyable trip across the Sound. It also opens up the prospect of circular tours through the splendours of Ardnamurchan and then over to Mull, and returning to Oban.

Back to the road, then, and you will find, as you pass through Kilchoan, a fork in the B8007. Go now on the road to the lighthouse. Before you reach the lighthouse, though, the road forks yet again. Keep right, through wild country, to the quite lovely beaches of Sanna, with their white sand, tidal pools, machair grass slopes and safe bathing. And, again, great panoramas of sea, islands and hills. It is a precious place, far from any rush or bustle.

It was to Sanna that many of the tenant farmers and peasants were driven when they were evicted from the rich lands further east around Swordle and Ockle. Heaven knows they could not have been driven any further without drowning, and the proprietors would not have worried if they had drowned. Those proprietors did not understand the doggedness of the people, though. Clearing stones off the little patches of land and building houses with those stones, they literally made paddocks, carrying seaweed and shell sand from the beaches. They learned to build boats and to fish, and they survived.

In the 1880's, during the near-insurrection of the Land League activities, the people of Western Ardnamurchan played a great and proud part. They never got back the land which had belonged to their fathers and their ancestors, but they did get security on the new fields they had made for themselves, and security for their houses.

If you take the left hand road where you forked right for Sanna, you come eventually to Ardnamurchan Point with its lighthouse. Like the road to Sanna, this is a very interesting journey, through some wild enough country, but also past green and fertile stretches.

Even those with no knowledge of the science will understand that to geologists this is a most fascinating area. Fifty or sixty million years ago, volcanoes vomited great masses of molten rock hereabouts. Beinn Hiant, regular and shapely, is one such extinct volcano. In other places, the soft outer skin of the volcano has weathered away, leaving us the hardened core, which was once molten, of tough gabbro rock. McLean's Nose, that cliff near Kilchoan, is one such. McLean's Nose is the solidified contents of a great volcanic cauldron, a Hell's Broth once bubbling and boiling, waiting for the next eruption. But that next eruption never came, and the molten rock slowly cooled and the cauldron itself disappeared, as wind and water gradually, over aeons of time, rasped it away, leaving behind the solidified contents for us to wonder about today.

Most of Ardnamurchan is volcanic in origin, and here and there it is shot through with pipes of minerals -- lead, copper, strontium and semi-precious stones. It is a strange land, one where the chaos of its creation can never be far from anyone's thoughts. It was written of another range of Scottish hills that it was: '.........a weird, wild world, new and strange, not yet out of chaos, not yet approved of God.' That perfectly describes Ardnamurchan Point.

The lighthouse, which is now automatic and unmanned, is a fine structure, standing strong and clean on a high cliff. One hundred and fourteen feet high, it is built of pinkish granite from the Ross of Mull, and there are one hundred and forty steps to the light chamber. The view from there is quite without compare, and would be a fitting climax to this tour of Ardnamurchan. But even from ground level, the world seems to be all sea and islands, brightly coloured, sparkling and vivid, almost new minted and still young and virginal. It is a world with all the brilliance of molten enamel and the pristine wonder of a spring day. Watch a sunset from there, and marvel at that crimson glory, and be glad that it lasts so brief a time, for such loveliness can be unbearable.

Even before the latest changes, the lighthouse had been modernised and mechanised, but there were still interesting old brass mechanisms in the lightroom, which used to drive the great light by gravity. Spruce and spartan and polished like a ship's bridge, it was a fine place to visit. And on the invitation of the keeper, you were always very welcome. It is too late now, though, for the lighthouse keepers have gone and there are plans to turn their houses into yet another Heritage Centre of some sort. There is a sundial there, and it shows the time as being twenty five minutes after Greenwich Mean Time. That tells you how far west you have come.

This tip of land, Ardnamurchan Point, once marked the dividing line between the Nordreys and the Sudreys That was a thousand years ago, and the Nordreys and the Sudreys have both gone into the mists of history. The Sudreys, though, are still remembered by the title of the Bishop of Sodor and Man, not that his See extends to the length of Ardnamurchan these days.

Almost a thousand years before that, Tacitus, the Roman historian, wrote of this land that:

"Nowhere has the sea a wider dominion; it has many currents running in every direction; it does not merely ebb and flow within the limits of the shores but penetrates and winds far inland, and finds a home among hills and mountains as though in its own domain."

Well said indeed, and a true description, although old Tacitus could never have seen what he described.

From all this way, you must now travel back by the same road. And although you may be tired, most certainly you will not be weary, for this road of romance, this road to the Isles, is unfailingly lovely and a track of true delight.

FORT WILLIAM, SPEAN BRIDGE, ROY BRIDGE, LOCH GARRY, LOCH HOURN.

The main road through the Great Glen between Fort William and Inverness is a major traffic artery, joining Scotland's east and west coasts. It is a busy road, and although much improved these days, does not give a lot of opportunity for looking around.

For many centuries the Great Glen has been a highway for traffic. Throughout all of history the lochs and tracks through the glen have witnessed the passage of goods, men, ideas and beliefs. To the Gael, the glen is Glen More nan Alba, the Great Glen of Alba and Alba was the ancient name for Scotland north of the Forth and the Clyde.

It provided relatively easy passage across the country, avoiding the problems of mountain passes and high peaks, and certainly it has had profound effects on the national development of the country. In the Stone Age the people who built the great chambered cairns of Argyll traversed it to reach the plains of the north and the north-east. Christianity travelled that route, too, as Columba and Moluag, from Iona and Lismore, spread their beliefs to the Pictish centre at what is now Inverness. Much later, it was an important route of communication between the two great strongholds of Celtic civilisation on the east and west as they fought to maintain themselves against the feudal and centralising policy of the Norman-infected feudal kings of the Canmore dynasty.

The Glen itself is a great ancient crack in the rock mantle of Scotland. Formed by some cataclysmic upheaval perhaps 300 million years ago, it is still not stable, and frequent earth tremors, particularly at Inverness, show that adjustments are taking place to this day. It must indeed have been a cataclysmic upheaval, for granite now found at Strontian is also found at Foyers, and that indicates a displacement of about 65 miles. More, Loch Ness is in part 774 feet deep and there are hills round the Loch well over 2000 feet high and that after the denudation of 300 million years. Some cataclysm: some cleft!

But all that was long ago: today the Great Glen is a grand chain of lochs running across almost the whole country, cradled by massive hills, and those hills are in turn divided by passes and glens running to the north and west, into the vast empty glory of the true Highlands, where we shall be travelling.

The Caledonian Canal runs through the Glen, using the lochs. Our journey starts where the Canal starts, by Banavie, where a complex series of locks carries the Canal up 64 feet. Collectively, the locks are known as Neptune's Staircase.

There is not much traffic through the Canal these days, and the little there is is mostly pleasure craft. It was not always so. The Canal is a short cut from east to west, and by using it vessels were saved the long and very hazardous journey right round the north of Scotland and through the treacherous Pentland Firth. Not so long ago, the great fishing fleets from Scotland's east coast used the Canal constantly to reach the fish-rich waters of the West. Today, the east coast boats tie up in the western ports, and the crews travel by road to their homes in the fishing villages of the east.

The Canal is just over 150 years old now. As with so much else in the Highlands, it goes back to Thomas Telford, that remarkable polymath of a man whose work in so many fields changed the course of Highland history. Telford was a stonemason from Dumfries-shire, totally self-taught, a poet and artist as well as engineer and architect. Working at a period when austerity and good proportions seemed almost innate in architects, he left a legacy of great value in his work, both engineering and building. Not that he was the first to envisage a canal across the waist of Scotland. Away back in the middle of the 17th century the Brahan Seer foretold it, and foretold many other things, too, which have also come to pass.

It was James Watt who first surveyed the route for the Canal, but the Government of his day shelved the report. Then in 1801 Telford was asked to report on the high level of emigration from the Highlands.

The Government was concerned, because the Highlander was the backbone of the British Army, and the young men were leaving the country in some considerable numbers for the excitement and adventure of the New World. Telford's report concluded that it was lack of work at the root of the problem. He proposed a large scheme of public works, including the Canal. His Report, incidentally, is almost as valid today as it was then. At that time, too, for it was during the Napoleonic Wars, French ships were harrassing British shipping round the north of Scotland, and it was obvious that a canal would remove that danger. So the work began in 1804, with Thomas Telford as consulting engineer at a salary of 3 guineas a day.

It was not easy, and nor was it cheap. There were all kinds of problems, both engineering and social. And of course financial, for the estimated costs rose steadily. However, it was completed in 1822, and in October of that year there was an official opening, with a convoy of celebrating VIPs travelling from Inverness to Fort William in two days. In spite of continuing engineering problems, the Canal was a commercial success, with 844 vessels using it in 1823, and in 1863 over 15,000 people passed through the Canal by steamer.

It is all very different today, when there is but little commercial traffic through the Canal. Just the same, travelling by water through the Great Glen is an unforgettable experience, and one can only applaud those wise enough to spend a holiday doing that. Apart from the privately owned boats, there are plenty of ways for the non-boat-owner to travel the Canal, and it is difficult to think of any more satisfying way to spend a vacation afloat.

The Brahan Seer, who foretold the canal so many years ago, was Kenneth Odhar Mackenzie, born about 1600 in Lewis, but who worked on the Brahan estate of the Seaforths. Somehow he had acquired a pierced blue stone, with which he was able to foretell the future, and many of his prophesies, indubitably recorded at the time, were most certainly fulfilled. His powers led to his own death. Once, when the Earl of Seaforth had been long months in Paris, Lady Seaforth called for the Seer, and asked him to find the whereabouts of her husband. Mackenzie looked into his stone, and told the Lady that her husband was well and happy. She pressed him for more details, and reluctantly he said that he saw the Earl kneeling before a beautiful lady and pressing his lips to her hand. In anger, Lady Seaforth ordered the execution of the Seer, in the best traditions of killing the bearer of bad news, and he was plunged into a barrel of burning tar. First, though, he foretold, in great detail, the end of the Seaforth line, and that most certainly came to pass.

It happens that the road (B8004) to Gairlochy runs alongside the western side of the Canal for several miles, and that here it is a real canal, not a loch. It is one of the few stretches where you can actually walk along canal banks, and it is something very much worth while doing. It is all very quiet and peaceful, and you can reflect on how the scars of this great work have healed, and of how what was once a great enterprise has again dwindled into insignificance, like so many other great enterprises in the Highlands.

This road along the western side of the Canal is a very pleasant alternative to at least the first part of the main A82. It runs through wooded country, with striking and unusual views back over the Ben Nevis massif, across the Great Glen. A very minor road runs off to the left, up Glen Loy, but peters out after about 3 miles.

Unless you are in a great hurry to get further north and west, there is an excellent side trip from Gairlochy along Loch Arkaig, on the B8005. This is about 18 miles of quite well-surfaced single track road with ample passing places. (Incidentally, almost all the roads recommended in this book can be so described: a striking contrast with the situation a few years ago.)

Before reaching Loch Arkaig, the road runs for a while along

LOCH ARKAIG

the west shore of Loch Lochy, past the entrance to Achnacarry House, and then turns eastwards through the strange Mille Dorcha.

Achnacarry House is the seat of Cameron of Locheil, a name that sounds down through much of Scottish history. It was the Locheil of his day who went to Glenfinnan on that fateful day in 1745 to persuade Prince Charles Edward to return to France. He failed in his persuasion and fell under the Prince's undoubted charismatic spell, and he and all his men fought through to Culloden. Afterwards, his house of Achnacarry was burned and all the Locheil lands confiscated. The house we see today replaced that burned by order of the Butcher Cumberland in 1746, but the ruins of the old house can still be traced just by the new house.

It was here at Achnacarry that the ancient right of 'pit and gallows' was last exercised. In the old days, the clan chiefs had a certain heritable jurisdiction, which meant that they held their own courts of justice and extorted their own punishments and very rough much of that justice was. The heritable jurisdictions were abolished after 1745, as part of the scheme to break up the clan society. However the writ of London did not carry much weight in the Highlands (at least not when it was inconvenient for the clan chiefs) and as late as 1754 an alleged cattle thief was hanged in summary justice on the gallows tree at Achnacarry.

From 1941 to 1945, Achnacarry was one of the two main centres for Commando and Combined Operations training. Those who experienced it are hardly likely to forget such delights as the Tarzan Course and the Death Ride, the demolition exercises and the night assault practices.

Today it is peaceful and lovely. The Mille Dorcha, or Dark Mile, a long, quiet avenue of beech trees, ancient and sleepy, is a grand road to walk. Just by Mille Dorcha is Cia-Aig, a rather ostentatious little torrent pouring off the steep hillside. There is a marked forest walk, through the hanging beech trees, all very fine and peaceful.

At the head of Loch Arkaig is Glendessary, and a track for

walking leads right through the Glen to the head of Loch Nevis and then onwards into the lonely and utter wilderness of Knoydart. It is not the sort of walking that should be tried as a Sunday afternoon stroll, but if you take that track it will lead you into very empty, very wild and very beautiful country.

The track, incidentally, was one of the roads cut by General Wade, and went as far as Loch Nevis. The plan for those roads was laid down after the 1715 Jacobite Rising, and they were designed to allow Government troops to move quickly through the Highlands. They did nothing to prevent or defeat the much bigger Rising of 1745.

If you do walk into Knoydart from Loch Arkaig, there are very reasonable tracks as far as Barrisdale, then along Loch Hourn to Kinlochourn, which is the end of a road leading from Invergarry. But if you do that, beware of the Bull of Barrisdale.That fearful beast has not been seen recently, but the legends about it are still fresh. It had (perhaps still has) only three legs, and each leg ended in a paw and a single claw. Its roar was like some great clap of thunder. The intrepid men of Barrisdale once followed its fresh tracks through a fall of snow, but when the tracks reached a sheer precipice they went straight up it. So, surely wisely, the gallant men of Barrisdale returned home.

Not surprisingly, the laird of Barrisdale was 'out' with the Jacobite Army in 1745. He was Colla Ban, or Handsome Coll. He was a good soldier, gallant in both field and boudoir, and was knighted by Prince Charles Edward after Prestonpans. Coll was on the run after Culloden, but was captured by the Hanoverians. He knew well that Prince Charles Edward was in the Hebrides, but he told his interrogators that the Prince was staying with a family of Campbells in Perthshire. As a reward for his 'information' Coll was released and again took to the hills, but when his information was shown to be false, Barrisdale House was burned down in revenge. Its ruins can still be seen near the new house.

That was not the end of it for Coll, though. He escaped to

France on a French man-o'-war, but was then imprisoned there by his Prince, who believed Coll to be plotting against him. Eventually he escaped, went to London, only to be imprisoned again there. Finally poor Handsome Coll died in prison in Edinburgh, but he is not forgotten, and even today there are arguments about his role in that Jacobite Rising. His son, incidentally, was also out and was captured after Culloden. At the age of 20 he was sentenced to be hanged, drawn and quartered, but the sentence was remitted. That remission was one of the arguments advanced that Handsome Coll was in fact a traitor to the Jacobite cause. Had the lad suffered the barbaric punishment, no doubt Handsome Coll would universally be accepted as another Jacobite patriot.

It was another laird of Barrisdale who lost the family lands. He quarrelled with an old woman who lived on the shore below Barrisdale House. The old woman made some sort of precarious living by collecting shell fish from the strand, but in his anger against her (legend does not tell us the cause of the quarrel) Barrisdale decreed that the strand be ploughed up. That was done, and of course it destroyed the old woman's livelihood. She cursed the Laird, in very explicit terms, prophesying that he would lose all his possessions, that his lands would be under the sea and his family forced to live on shellfish. And so it happened. There was a great storm, and the waters of Loch Hourn flooded over the Barrisdale lands. All the Laird's wealth was lost, and he and his family forced for weeks on end to live on whatever they could gather from the shore, and finally they left, never to return. The moral, so far as there is one, is that you should never quarrel with old women in the Highlands!

Loch Arkaig has for centuries been the home of a water horse, although it has not been seen in recent years. Just to be safe, though, do not be tempted to steal a ride on any horse you might see in the district: it just might be the Each uisge, and you could end up lost forever under the still waters of the Loch.

There is another famous white horse of legend from Glen

Dessary. Jenny Cameron of the Glen rode over the hills to Glenfinnan to meet Prince Charles Edward in 1745, wearing a green jacket and riding a white horse, with the men of the Glen following her. She was at the raising of the Standard there at Glenfinnan, but did not ride south with the Jacobite Army and her Prince.

From the shore of Loch Arkaig it is necessary to go back to Gairlochy and the B8004, and from the foot of Loch Lochy climb up through some mature woods on the very pleasant road which joins the A82 Fort William Inverness road just by the Commando Memorial.

That heroic piece of sculpture stands in a very commanding position, looking out over many miles of moor, mountain and loch. It was over those lovely but barren lands that so many Commandoes learned their fearful trade, which led, all too often, only to death. The monument was made by Scott Sutherland, and unveiled by the Queen in 1952.

For an interesting side trip, before continuing for the north and west, the Parallel roads of Glen Roy are very much worth seeing. From the Commando Memorial continue east along A82 a very short way to its junction with the A86. Follow that road for just over a mile, then take the unclassified road to the left up Glen Roy, at Roy Bridge.

You can't miss seeing the Parallel Roads, which of course are not roads at all but are raised beaches 7 miles long and absolutely horizontal, formed by successive levels of a great glacial lake which once filled the Glen. But they look like roads, following every twist and turn and recess of the hills, and even snaking concentrically round Bohuntine Hill on the valley floor. They are grass covered, and very clear on the heather slopes.

This whole area so far talked about is extremely interesting from many points of view. It has great beauty and quietness; there is much history here and legend. And yet it is by no means remote. The roads are good and the walks many. Altogether, it could be an excellent area for a holiday.

Back, then, to the main road, the A82 to the north along Loch Lochy. There is no alternative here to the main road, but you wouldn't really want one, for the main road is grand and very satisfying. It runs for miles alongside the Loch, with fine views across to the heights of Meall Coire nan Saobhaidh and Sron a Choire Ghairbh.

Although there is no public road along the west side of Loch Lochy, there are some tracks, and one leads right through the pass between those great mountains. From the head of the pass there is a scene of magnificence, with all the glory of the Highlands there in abundance. There are immense views in every direction. This is Drumalbin, the stony backbone of Scotland, which runs all the miles from Ardgour by Fort William to Ben Hope at Loch Erribol in the distant north. From where you stand on that pass between the two mountains you can gather something of its vastness and its grandeur.

A little further north, just past the Laggan Swing Bridge over the Canal, is a strange monument, known as the Well of the Seven Heads. The monument itself is not the well, which is today buried by the road. There are inscriptions in Gaelic, English, French and Latin, surmounted by carvings of the heads of seven men. This commemorates 'the swift course of feudal justice' when seven brothers were alleged to have killed the Chief of Keppoch and his brother, apparently in hope of inheriting the position themselves. But instead they were themselves killed, in an ambush organised by the Bard of the dead chief. It was not enough to be a poet in those days; you also had to be a warrior. The Bard washed the heads in this well, and presented them to the Chief of Glengarry.

The strangely pompous and ostentatious monument was erected in 1852 by Col. Alister Ronaldson Macdonnel of Glengarry, who was the last of his line to own the ancestral lands, and who never travelled anywhere without his 'tail' of armed and kilted Highlanders. He was a friend of Sir Walter Scott, and it is believed that the character of Fergus Maciver in Waverley is based on the good Colonel. It would be interesting to know whether Sir Walter's misty and romantic view of the Highlands was influenced by the Colonel, or whether the Colonel was influenced by Sir Walter in his search for a heroic past that never truly existed.

At Invergarry you will take the A87, the road to the north and west, leaving the A82 to go off along the course of the Canal and the length of Loch Ness to Inverness.

The A87 begins by travelling a mile or so along Loch Garry, before turning northwards, but a very fine minor road goes straight ahead along the north side of Loch Garry. This narrow unclassifed road goes all the way back to the west coast, at the head of Loch Hourn in Knoydart. Loch Garry and Loch Quoich are part of an elaborate hydro-electric system, and there are dams and power stations. But don't let that put you off travelling the road, for they are not blots on the landscape, and if they were not there, probably the road would not exist. As a matter of fact, the hydro-electric scheme here has vastly changed the scenery, and not for the worse. Loch Garry itself is about twice its original length because of dams and the great dam at Loch Quoich is itself worth journeying to see.

It is hardly surprising that this particular area has been chosen

for an elaborate hydro system, because the rainfall hereabout is over 200 inches each year, one of the highest in the Highlands. The works were completed some years ago, and the scars have long healed, and today the transformed lochs lie quietly in great beauty. Travelling westwards on that road one cannot escape -- and who would wish to? -- the great louring mountains of Knoydart ahead. Of course you must go back the way you came, to the A87, but that road along the lochs is very fine indeed.

Perhaps one of the best views of Loch Garry and distant Knoydart is from a marked viewpoint on the A87, where the road has left the loch and climbed steeply on its way north to Loch Loyne. From that position the view is open for miles down Loch Garry, and it is a very fine panorama.

BEN NEVIS

LOCH CLUANIE, GLEN SHIEL, LOCH DUICH, GLENELG, ARNISDALE, EILEAN DONAN, KYLE OF LOCHALSH

The road past Loch Cluanie (A87) is usually thought of as the Road to the Isles, and indeed it leads to Lochalsh, where a very busy ferry crosses to Skye. But it is not the road of the deservedly popular song. That is to the south, '*by Morar to the sea.*' This road past Loch Cluanie is a grand road, though, with much of the romance and tragedy of the Highlands along its length.

Loch Cluanie (the Loch of the Meadows) has no meadows on its shores now. They vanished when the level of the loch was raised when it was dammed for the hydro-electric scheme. The road along its northern shore has been changed and now runs higher up the hills than in the past. It is none the worse for that: the distant views are better.

Glen Moriston, where Loch Cluanie begins, is rich in memories of Prince Charles Edward and the Jacobite Rising of 1745. It was here that Roderick Mackenzie died at the hands of the Redcoats, and by his death helped to ensure that the Prince escaped.

Young Mackenzie was the son of an Edinburgh jeweller, and was an ardent and courageous Jacobite. It happened that he had a superficial resemblance to Prince Charles Edward, and this amused the Prince, who appointed Roderick as one of his personal bodyguards. After Culloden, in those desperate days when the Prince was striving to win his way to the west and a ship for France, he wandered these hills for weeks, protected by men of Glen Moriston. For part of the time they stayed in a cave at Corridoe.

It appears that the garrison at Fort Augustus suspected that Charles was somewhere in the district, and patrols and search parties constantly combed the area. One party came across young Roderick, himself a fugitive and striving to win to the west. Instead of running, as he could well have done, and instead of escaping as he may have done, Roderick stood and fought, and was shot. Virtually with his last breath he called out ' *You have killed your Prince.* '

The patrol, deceived by the words and the resemblance, were sure that they had killed the Prince, and no doubt were already thinking of how they would spend that £30,000 reward. They cut the head off the body, and carried it proudly back to Fort Augustus.

It happened that Cumberland, the Butcher in command of the Hanoverian forces, was there, and he was doubtful about the head. Certainly it looked like the Prince, but he was not quite certain. So messengers were sent off to London, carrying their grisly burden, in hope that someone there could say positively *yea* or *nay* about that head. But there was no-one in London able to do that. Only one man, it was thought, could be certain, and that was Peter Morrison, the Prince's batman, and he was lying in Carlisle Castle, awaiting execution. So Peter Morrison was sent for, but it was too late: the head was far too decayed for identification.

Something good did come out of it, for Peter Morrison's sentence was commuted, and eventually he was freed. Roderick Mackenzie, meanwhile, lies in a quiet grave just off the A887 two miles or so past its junction with the A87 on the road to Invermoriston. There is a memorial to that very gallant young man by the grave. It is not so easy to find, but if you take the first lane to the right on A887, you will see the memorial on your left in about 100 yards.

The sacrifice made by Roderick Mackenzie was not a vain one, for Cumberland himself had been half convinced by the severed head, and he left for London and the fleshpots he so sorely missed. With the Butcher gone, the vigilance and enthusiasm of the troops was lessened, and Prince Charles Edward was able to break through and win to the west.

As mentioned earlier, at this period in his wanderings, the Prince was guarded and sheltered by the men of Glen Moriston. It was in July 1746 that the Prince reached Glen Moriston, hiding by day and moving by night, and he was exhausted. He sought refuge in a hut there, desperate for rest and shelter. There were eight men in the hut, outlaws like himself, and one recognised him. The rest had to be told, although they were not fugitives from Culloden, but just thieves and vagabonds. Nevertheless, they swore a mighty oath that they would protect and help their Prince.

They did, moving him slowly westwards, hiding in huts and caves, until finally they delivered him to Locheil, his friend. On one occasion, legend has it, the Prince was reminiscing about the past, and remarked that one thing he greatly missed was gingerbread. One of the men risked passing through the Redcoat patrols and went into Fort Augustus to buy a pennysworth of gingerbread for the Prince's pleasure.

There were two MacDonalds in the group, three Chisholms, a McGregor, a Grant and a McMillan. Years later, one of them, Hugh Chisholm, still lived in Edinburgh, an old man and a poor one, but he refused to shake hands with his right hand, for Prince Charles had shaken that hand, and no one was fit to follow him.

At the same time as that, of course, his Prince, a bloated drunkard, was living a high life in Rome.

That road along Loch Cluanie goes beneath grand hills, several of them over the 3000 feet mark, and just past the Loch it climbs up to the water shed before the dramatic drop down through Glen Shiel to Loch Duich.

It was somewhere in Glen Shiel that one of the best known books in the English language was conceived. Dr. Samuel Johnson and his devoted amenuensis James Boswell travelled through the Glen on 1st September 1773, and Johnson recorded that they stoppped at one point to rest and feed the horses. In his usual verbose fashion, the irascible old writer reported that:

" *The day was calm, the air soft, and all was rudeness, silence and solitude. Before me, on either side, were high hills, which by hindering the eye from ranging, forced the mind to find entertainment for itself. Whether I spent the hour well I know not, for here I first conceived the thought of this narration.* "

And thus was born his *Journey to the Western Isles*, a book still an excellent companion to any traveller in these parts.

It was Boswell, not Johnson, who recorded their stay at the village of Auchnashiel which was somewhere here, but has now disappeared. They took refreshment there, at one of the houses, and distributed coppers to the natives, not one of whom could speak English. Boswell remarked that it was like being amongst a tribe of Indians, and Johnson agreed, although he thought it not so terrifying. They agreed on that, but Johnson had the last word (he usually did) when Boswell thought that a particular mountain was immense. Johnson denied that, and said that it was no more than 'a considerable protuberance'.

Certainly whether you hold the mountains to be immense or merely considerable protuberances, there are many of them. For myself, I hold them to be immense, and anyone who differs is being pedantic, as of course Johnson was, almost impossibly so.

It was here in Glen Shiel, under the massive shoulders of the Five Sisters of Kintail, that the Jacobite Uprising of 1719 blazed so briefly. It is often forgotten that there was a rising in 1719, although those of 1715 and 1745 are well enough known.

Sir Walter Scott, who travelled these roads, called 1719 'the last faint sparkle of the Great Rebellion of 1715.' In a sense, that faint sparkle came from the ambitions of Spain in Europe, for the rising was encouraged and financed by the Spanish as a means of distracting English attention. They loaned ships and men, and two Spanish frigates landed a force of 300 soldiers and arms for 2000 men at Castle Eilean Donan at the foot of Loch Duich. With the Spanish were the Earl Marischal and the Earl of Seaforth and the Marquis of Tullibardine, and they were soon joined by Seaforth's men, but not by others, for the fiasco of 1715 had not been forgotten, and nor had the less than valiant role played by James Stuart, the King over the Water.

In fact, an earlier rising had been planned for 1717, but English spies had learned of that, and the Spanish knew that the English knew, so it was postponed, but in 1719 a very elaborate plan was under way, of which the uprising in the Highlands was no more than a diversion. There was to be an invasion of the west of England by Spain and Sweden, and James Stuart -- King James -- was invited to join this. Typically, he literally missed the boat, and the fleet sailed without him, only to meet one of the notorious Biscay gales and be almost totally lost. They did not know that an English fleet was waiting for them, anyway.

The Spanish ships heading for Scotland survived the storm and evaded the English, and eventually reached the Hebrides. Men from the Highlands and the Islands joined the Jacobite Standard when it was raised, but not very many, and after a while the mainland base was established at Eilean Donan, the stronghold of the Earl of Seaforth. The English were following close, though, and a naval squadron sailed into the Kyle of Lochalsh and bombarded Eilean Donan castle from the sea. Its Spanish garrison, without adequate artillery, could do nothing, and surrendered on May 9th, and the castle was blown up.

Meanwhile the morale of the Highlanders was very low, for they had learned of the fate of the expedition to the West of England. The remaining Spaniards and the Highland men retreated up Glen Shiel, but on 10th May they were brought to battle by General Wightman, who had marched his motley army of English, Germans and some Scots up from Inverness. It was a confused battle, but the result was conclusive enough. The Jacobite force was routed. The Spaniards fought well, and indeed offered to continue, but the Highlanders melted away into the hills and the mists.

Wightman, in the usual way, rampaged through the country, burning, looting and killing, but there was a sequel.

It is believed that many of the arms brought by the Spaniards were buried in the hills and later, in 1745, were brought into good use.

Three months later the dilatory James Stuart married Princess Clementina Sobieski, and in the summer of the next year she bore a son, Charles Edward, the Bonny Prince Charles of legend. The boy's father never saw England or Scotland again, and gave no one the chance of collecting the £100,000 price put on his head, but Prince Charles Edward later spent some time as a fugitive in that same Glen Shiel.

There were some legendary consequences of that rather ridiculous and abortive Rising. The Earl of Seaforth escaped, wounded, and went to Spain, but his lands and his title were forfeited. During those long years of exile, his estates were supposed to be managed by the Commissioners of the Forfeited Estates, who were to have the benefit of the rents from the tenantry. It did not work out like that, though. Kintail is wild country, far from the seat of Government, and the law's writ was not powerful there. In fact, the rents were collected by Seaforth's factor, Donald Murchison for the Earl himself, and Murchison made several dangerous journeys to France to deliver the money to his Earl.

On one occasion a military expedition was mounted to help the Commissioners in their attempts to collect the rents, but it was ambushed and driven back by Murchison and the Macraes somewhere in the wild country by Glen Affric. In truth, Kintail was a 'no-go area'.

However, the Government had a stroke of luck, for on one occasion when Murchison was returning from the Continent, his ship was captured, and he was imprisoned in the Tower. That was in the mid-1720s, when there was a strong move to have the exiled Highlanders pardoned and their forfeited estates returned. The King himself, George I, visited Murchison in the Tower, and was impressed by his loyalty to his Chief. He offered to pardon Murchison if he would swear that in future he would give as much loyalty to the King as he had given to his Chief. Well aware of the moves to grant a general pardon, Murchison agreed, and was released, to make his way home with the gift of a grant of land from the King.

Soon afterwards, Seaforth returned, but quite failed to show Murchison the gratitude that surely was his right. Seaforth was perhaps jealous of his factor's power and popularity, and even refused to recognise the grant of land made by the King. Deeply wounded by his Chief's ingratitude, Donald Murchison retired to the east, and soon died, a sad and embittered man.

All in all, the Earls of Seaforth were not a happy lot. They owed their power originally to King Robert Bruce, whom they supported, and who was once entertained at Eilean Donan castle. Always strong supporters of the Stuarts, the second Earl was excommunicated after the Covenanting Wars. The third Earl was with King Charles at the Battle of Worcester, and was captured and imprisoned. Cromwell explicitly excluded him from the Grace and Pardon Act of 1654. The fourth Earl followed the deposed James VII to France and when he returned to Scotland was one of those defeated by General MacKay in 1690. He was imprisoned for seven years in Edinburgh. The fifth Earl fought with the Old Pretender in 1715, escaped to France, returned for the shambles of the 1719 rising, and was wounded and exiled.

The title is now extinct, and the Brahan Seer foretold that long before it happened. He foretold it just before his execution at the order of Lady Seaforth. He prophesied that an Earl of Seaforth would one day find that of his four neighbours one would be buck-toothed, one hare-lipped, one half-witted and one a stammerer. When that happened, Seaforth would know that his sons would die before him, that his heir would be a 'white-coiffed lass' from the east who had killed her sister, and that the Seaforth line would end with her, and that all the Seaforth lands would pass into the hands of strangers.

And it all happened like that. Mackenzie of Gairloch, The Chisholm, Grant and Raasay had the disabilities described; two of

THE ROARING STAG

Seaforth's sons died and finally the third, a weakling, died in August
1814. The father died a few months later, and the heir was a young
widow (white-coiffed) who had recently returned from India, and
who had been driving with her sister when the horses ran away and
the sister was thrown out of the carriage and killed. The line of the
Seaforths ended with the young widow, who was childless.

With such a record of successful prophesy, you will understand
why many people take very seriously those of the Seer's prophesies
which have not yet come to pass, some of which are quite horrifying.

The road between Lochs Cluanie and Duich (named after St.
Dubthach, in the 11th century) is one of continuous splendour, with

FALLS OF GLOMACH

vast mountains on each side, mountains whose Gaelic names are like great chords of music.

A large part of this area, Kintail, is in the charge of the National Trust for Scotland, and consequently visitors are positively encouraged to walk the hills and glens and very fine walking they are too.

About 12,800 acres of this magnificent countryside hereabouts is now owned by the National Trust for Scotland, and that includes the Five Sisters. Those stupendous grass-covered mountains springing so steeply from sea level to almost 3000 feet are always impressive, even from the roadside. How much more so when walking them!

The National Trust for Scotland information centre at Morvich, at the head of Loch Duich, will provide detailed information on walks in Kintail and that advice should always be sought. They can recommend something for everyone.

The walk up Gleann Choinneachain is grand. A big burn tumbles down from the glen on the north side of Beinn Fhada (or Ben Attow, your map might claim), in a series of exhilarating torrents and rock pools, and following its course is always a delight. One of the finest walks, though, is to the Falls of Glomach. This highly dramatic cascade is one of the highest in Britain. The Gaelic name Glomach means 'forbidding', and this the falls are. There is a sheer drop of almost 300 feet, and then a further drop of 50 feet to a pool, with the stream approaching the lip of the fall through a wild ravine, and then twisting away from the foot of the falls in a narrow, boiling torrent. The whole scene is magnificent in its wildness, and more than worth the walking to get there, for walk you must.

Actually, there are several approachs on foot, of which the shortest is a bare five miles by well-marked track from Glen Elchaig, which you reach by driving along the very attractive minor road along the west side of Loch Long. But the finest and most dramatic approach is from the bridge across the river at the head of Loch Duich. To get there, you follow the old road right round the head of the Loch, not crossing the new causeway. A foot track from the bridge leads to Dorusduain, where the track divides. Both arms will lead you to the Falls. The left hand track goes first through Forestry Commission plantations, which are not particularly interesting, before reaching open country and climbing quite steeply to about 1700 feet to cross the Beallach na Sroine (Pass of the Nose) between the great hills A Glas Bheinn and Beinn Bhreac. It then dips smartly to the Falls.

The other track, the right hand branch at Dorusduain, is surely the best, although it is a longer walk. It heads south at first, and then east to Loch a Bhealaich, but to reach the loch you first go through the dramatic narrow Glen Gniomhaidh and on to the flanks of Beinn Fhada, which your map may show as Ben Attow. It then goes through the Rumbling Pass (Beallach am Sgairne) and further to the head of Loch a Bhealaich. There you leave the track, which wanders on into the lonely magnificence of Glen Affric.

For the Falls, though, you leave the track and strike across country, following the Loch (but keep it on your right). It can be a bit wet and rough, but the Loch shore is not too difficult. Actually, there is a little chain of lochs, connected by lanes (of water, not road), and it is from these that the Falls of Glomach originate. After you leave the lochs, the burn twists away northwards to disappear abruptly over the rim of the ravine at the head of the Falls. If there is a spate, you will hear the roaring and see the cloud of spray long before you reach the rim. Altogether a very fine and satisfying expedition on foot.

For the bird watcher, too, that could make a memorable day. In those mountains, of course, there is always a chance of seeing a golden eagle, and many buzzards and ravens on the quiet rock faces. Black-throated divers breed on the little chain of lochans above the Falls of Glomach, and the moors around those lochans are a favourite of greenshanks.

Before continuing north and west along the shore of Loch Duich, a side-trip to Glenelg is most highly recommended. For this, take the minor road to the left at Shiel Bridge at the head of the Loch.

That minor road runs right along the shore to its end at Totaig, five miles away, and gives grand views across the Loch, and eventually of Eilean Donan Castle, although you cannot reach the castle from the west shore line.

You can reach a quite interesting broch by a foot track beyond Totaig. This Caisteal Gragaig, is unique in that it was built from very large stones, and has walls nine feet thick. Especially noticeable is the massive triangular lintel above the entrance.

If you take the road on the left about a mile from where you left the main road, then you embark on the Mam Ratagan Pass. Sadly, it is but a shadow of what it once was. Forestry planting today hides what used to be extraordinary and dramatic views back over Loch Duich. It is still a considerable pass, and from the top you can stop and enjoy the grandeur of the view. It is from here that Kintail's Five Sisters are seen at their best, across the loch. One would like to think that today the forestry industry would have a little more foresight and sensitivity than to blank out some of the most splendid views in Scotland with miserable ranks of conifers, marching in their monotony down to the roadside. One would also like to think that that when these existing trees are cleared there can be some imaginative planting, leaving open vistas and using trees to enhance, not destroy, the beauty of the countryside.

The Mam Ratagan Pass climbs 1200 feet from sea level, and even today is a stiff climb. It was worse for Dr. Johnson and his friend Boswell. It is recorded that when climbing the Pass on their way to Skye, Johnson's horse staggered -- not surprising with the weight of the good Doctor -- and, surveying the precipitous fall all around him, this was the only moment in the whole long journey when Johnson felt himself in danger.

From the peak of the Pass, the road runs down through open country to Glen More. This is crofting country, and much of it is still worked in the old ways. Hay is put up on fences to dry, corn stooked, turnips and potatoes clamped. It is all desperately hard work, and work that brings little financial return these days. Not surprisingly, many of the crofts are no longer worked, and have reverted to waste land. Not surprising, perhaps, but very saddening to see good land going back to wilderness, especially when it is remembered how and why those crofts were made in the first place, by the sheer guts, strength and determination of those, two hundred years ago, who were driven ruthlessly off their ancestral lands to make way for the White Plague of sheep.

Glen More is blessed with a richness of foot tracks running into quiet and lonely country. Glenelg faces Skye, separated only by the narrow Kyle Rhea, and it was here that cattle from the island swam across to the mainland to begin the long trek southwards to the great cattle markets which supplied the English towns and cities. As many as 8000 cattle left Skye each year for the Tryst at Falkirk, and they were joined in that long trek by cattle from every island and glen in the north of Scotland. In those days, the glens and straths of the north were populated and prosperous enough: today they lie empty and desolate, a fact that must always cast a shadow on the whole-hearted delight at their beauty.

The name 'Glenelg' is a palindrome, that is, it reads the same backwards and forwards, and is the only one I know in Scotland. It reminds me always of what is claimed to have been the first palindrome ever spoken, the first words of Adam to Eve: *'Madam, I'm Adam.'*

Bernera Barracks are at Glenelg. They were built by the Government after the Rising of 1719 as part of the garrisoning of the Highlands, but in truth they were hardly successful. In 1745, the French ship that landed Prince Charles Edward at Moidart sailed up the Sound of Sleat, through Kyle Rhea to Glenelg and captured four English supply ships anchored there. There was nothing the Redcoat garrison could do -- they had no artillery.

Sir John MacDonald of Sleat died in Bernera Baracks in 1746, one of the most hated men in the Highlands, so hated that he felt safe only when surrounded by Hanoverian soldiers. He was convinced that the Jacobite cause was hopeless, and he gave full support to the Hanoverians. He caught pneunomia and died, and his suggested epitaph spread the breadth of the Highlands:

If Heaven be pleased when sinners cease to sin,
If Hell be pleased when sinners enter in,
If Earth be pleased to quit a truckling knave,
Then all are pleased
MacDonald's in his grave!

Later, in the 1830's, the Barracks saw even more dramatic events. Clearances came to Glenelg, and the people were evicted from their holdings. In despair, they gathered at the Barracks, long deserted by that time, and squatted there. That did not suit the book of the factor: he wanted them out of the district, whether to Glasgow, Canada or six feet underground was immaterial to him.

So the people were evicted from the Barracks and the building burned. Today we see only the roofless shell, but it is a sad place even now.

In those days, when the Barracks were burned, Glenelg was a populous place, with over 1100 people living in the district, many times the number living there today. But the Clearances dispersed them, to death or to new lives in strange and hostile countries.

Today Glenelg is a delightful small village looking out to Skye with its great louring peaks. The road to Glenelg and beyond to Arnisdale is a dead end, but it is a trip very much worth making. There is an airiness and quality of light there that is very strange and lovely.

Nearby is Kyle Rhea, where in the summer a car ferry crosses the narrow strait to Skye. It is well worth considering as an alternative to the very busy Kyle of Lochalsh ferry.

Beyond Glenelg the road continues for several miles right down to Arnisdale, and a side road to the left leads up Gleann Beag to the Glenelg Brochs.

These are splendid examples of Pictish construction, and in

themselves more than worth travelling this road. Built perhaps 2000 years ago, probably as a fortress and defensive position for all the families in the district, they are superb examples of the skills and architectural sophistication of that mysterious people.

They are round towers, and in the central courtyard it is believed that there were wooden huts to shelter the people and perhaps the animals. The walls are double-skinned, and between the skins are labyrinthine passages and stairways and alcoves ideal for defence against any enemy who may have broken through the narrow and stone-obstructed doorway. The inner skin of the wall is perpendicular, but the outer skin has most beautiful, sophisticated, almost sensuous, curves.

Even today there are many unanswered questions about these Scottish brochs. There are about 500 of them still visible, mostly in the north, and they are dated as 'Iron Age', which here in Scotland means the vast period between about 450BC and 400AD. They are mostly near the shore line -- the Glenelg ones are an exception -- and, it would seem from their distribution, (near the route that would be taken by marauders from Norway) were probably built as defensive strong points against Viking raiders. Although so strong, they could never have withstood a lengthy seige, which indicates that they were designed to protect against hit-and-run raiders, and this in turn indicates that the Norsemen were raiding these coasts perhaps as long as 800 years before they began settling.

Unfortunately the barbarians who built Bernera Baraacks 1700 years after the Picts built their brochs used the brochs as a convenient source of ready-quarried stone, and the top sections are missing. However, enough is left to leave everyone with a deep feeling of awe and wonder that those primitive people of whom we know so little had such skill in working those hard and stubborn stones.

The road south from Glenelg to Arnisdale (which is almost the end of the road) is very fine indeed, and there is one particular viewpoint at the top of the steep climb beyond the road to the brochs that gives an almost unparalleled vista of sea and mountain, out over the Sound of Sleat to Skye.

The road from there then runs on down the coast, and passes the side road to Sandaig, which was the *Camus Fearna* of Gavin Maxwell's books, in which he not only so brilliantly evoked the place he loved, but laid bare his own uneasy soul.

All of this, sadly, was Clearance country, and at the Government Enquiry which led directly to the first Crofting Act of 1886, much evidence was given of the misery of life here after the people had been cleared off their land to allow the formation of a great sheep farm. Arnisdale was a crofting/fishing village, peopled by those tenant farmers disposessed by the proprietors. Thirty thousand barrels of herring a year left Arnisdale, but when the fishing failed there was great distress, for the crofts were small and poor. The potatoes failed, too, and as a final blow a typhus epidemic swept the village, brought by a sailor home on leave from foreign parts.

The proprietor of old, Lord Glenelg, had sold up and gone, and his successor was one Baillie of Dochfour, and the whole vast area was converted into one great sheep farm. The Government Enquiry heard much criticism of Baillie and his factor George France. They had left the crofters so little grazing land that there was only one cow amongst 26 families. The crofters had complained about being forced to have their houses at Camus Ban, which was frequently flooded by high tides. France had suggested that they should build back doors to their houses the better to escape when the tide ran high! France also had the monopoly of barrels and salt for the herring, and waxed rich from his monopolies and the misery of the people.

The views south from Arnisdale to Knoydart are especially fine, with the great peak of Ladhar Bheinn dominating. A rough foot track from Corran, the end of the road, just beyond Arnisdale, leads for a further four miles along Loch Hourn, and gives magnificent views across the Loch to the wilderness of Knoydart, dominated by the great corries of Ladhar Bheinn. Looking to the west the great peaks of the Black Cuillin on Skye overshadow all else.

Barrisdale Bay, and Barrisdale House are there in Knoydart, and it was there that Coll MacDonnell lived in the mid-17th. century. He was the quintessential rogue, the model upon which all Godfathers and other Mafia hoodlums might be based. He appeared to be a fine gentleman, and mixed in the best circles. His behaviour was polished and his address cultured. In fact, his wealth came from the protection racket and from blackmail. He extorted payments from all around in return for 'protecting' their cattle and goods. He was often paid in black meal, the meal made from the barley grown in those days, and the only means of exchange in a society virtually cash-free. From 'blackmeal' came our modern word 'blackmail'. For those who did not wish to pay, there was always the Barrisdale, an instrument of torture invented by the estimable Coll, on which the victim was slowly screwed forward on to a steel spike.

Apart from the depredations of Coll MacDonnell, Knoydart suffered badly from all the MacDonnells of Glengarry. As early as 1770 that remote and lovely peninsula was being cleared of all its people, who were 'encouraged' to emigrate. The good agricultural land and the summer grazings went into sheep farms. But the MacDonnells were hard to satisfy, and eventually sold off the land to one James Baird, a sheep farmer from the Lowlands. A condition of the sale contract was that the MacDonnells had to evict all remaining tenants, and that was done with force and rigour, and the people driven off their holdings and from their burning houses.

Today, in all that 100 or so square miles there is a mere handful of people. Of course the sheep too have long gone, and that lovely country of hills and lochs, glens and beaches is empty, desolate and virtually unreachable, a classic example of a man-made wilderness.

Somehow, though, Knoydart does not rest quietly: there is always something happening about it. As recently as 1982 it was rescued from an attempt to make it yet another military training area. In 1948 it was the scene of the last land-raid in Scotland (at least the last so far) when ex-servicemen, hungry for workable land, staked claims in Knoydart, which then belonged to the pro-Nazi Lord Brockett. They received no encouragement from the Labour Government, and had to vacate their claims.

From Arnisdale you must take the same road back to Shiel Bridge and the head of Loch Duich, but it is a grand and fascinating road, and quite certainly you will not be bored by it.

Shiel House used to be an inn, a King's House, built to serve those travelling the new military road to Glenelg and Bernera Barracks. It was not a very good inn, and had only one room for the accommodation of all those unfortunate enough to stay there. Its main fame was the number and virulence of its bedbugs. James Hogg, the Ettrick Shepherd, that grand Lowland poet, once stayed there, and he recorded that, apart from the bugs, his rest was disturbed by a band of roistering Gaelic-speaking Highlanders who tried to rifle his pockets.

All of this land was once owned by the Mackenzies of Seaforth, and to give them their due, they stoutly resisted all temptations to clear the people off their lands, in spite of the high rents offered for sheep farms. However, when the last Earl died, those who inherited had no qualms, and very ruthlessly proceeded with the clearances, and the people who chose to stay in their native land were herded to the inhospitable shores and denuded of the grazings which alone made their way of life viable.

When wool prices fell, (chiefly due to cheap imports from Australia and New Zealand, where the descendents of many of those cleared from the Highlands were themselves now sheep farmers) the economic basis of the Highlands changed yet again, and the sheep farms themselves disappeared, and the whole vast area became deer forests. That land which had been denuded of people and trees for the sheep was now denuded of sheep for the deer.

In the 1880's there were 200 deer forests in the north of Scotland, three and a half million acres of them, one sixth of the whole land area of the country. In 1880, 200,000 acres were bought by an American, Louis Winans, a railway king, who had laid rails across both Russia and America. No 'sportsman' himself, his sole interest was in acquiring land and clearing everyone off it. The local minister said of his efforts in Kintail: 'Glen after glen is being cleared of its shepherd families, who are replaced by one or two solitary game watchers or "stoppers", who are usually the idlest of people pretending to earn a living, and the best customers of the adjacent public houses and shebeens.'

There was the quite hilarious episode of the Pet Lamb of Kintail, hilarious enough, but an episode that played no small part in the eventual passing of the Crofting Act of 1886.

Murdo Macrae was the cobbler at Carn Gorm, a harmless enough man, certainly no militant, but equally very stubborn. He reared a stray lamb, which grazed around the cobbler's workshop. One day one of Winan's keepers saw the lamb grazing a few feet off the public road and on Winan's land. He reported this, and Winan, a most litigious person, decided to prosecute the cobbler for allowing his lamb to trespass. The Sheriff Substitute at Dingwall decided in Murdo Macrae's favour, but Winan appealed to the Sheriff-Principal, who found in his favour. By now the whole affair had become a *cause célèbre* and Macrae attracted much support. At that time, the whole of the Islands and Highlands was in a considerable uproar over the question of the right of tenure for crofters, an uproar so great that gunboats were patrolling and troops ready to disperse rioters.

MacRae was able to carry his appeal to the Court of Session in Edinburgh, the pinnacle of Scottish law. There was a unanimous decision against Winan, and the Lord Chief Justice Clerk made some very biting remarks about him. Winan talked of appealing to the House of Lords, but did not do so, and as a final gesture of his anger had all the deer driven away from Kintail to the eastern side of his vast estate. Within a week all the deer from the whole estate are said to have been back in Kintail, while the men of Loch Duich acted as though they had nothing to do with that strange migration.

The whole story passed into Highland folklore, but it was also quoted as an example of proprietorial arrogance to the Commission from which sprang the Crofting Act in 1886.

There is a choice of roads towards the end of Loch Duich when travelling north-west. A minor road, signposted Carrbrae, goes steeply up the hill on the right, and I think it is worth taking for the sudden dramatic sight of Eilean Donan Castle. The new road, smooth and fast, is good, but the minor road is fine.

This, not so many years ago, was the major road, and all the traffic to and from Skye travelled it. That is hard to believe today.

Eilean Donan castle is perhaps the most photographed place in all of Scotland, and in spite of the chocolate-box associations, its grandeur never fails to give a frisson of delight.

On a small off-shore island where Lochs Duich, Alsh and Long meet, the castle dominated much of the sea traffic in these waters. Like others up and down this glorious coast of mountains and fiords, that was its purpose, for in those days communication was by the sea, not across the land, and threats, from whichever quarter, came from the sea.

The castle gets its name from Donnan, one-time abbot of Eigg, and another great proselytiser in the north. On Easter Day, 617AD, he was celebrating Mass on the shore of Loch Duich, with fifty-two monks and a lot of new converts, when the Norsemen arrived. Donnan refused to run, and the Norsemen, impressed, gave him leave to complete his devotions before being killed. Donnan finished his Mass, and he and the other monks were promptly beheaded.

The castle we see today is modern, and was built this century, although that is hard to believe at first sight, for the restoration has been carried out so skilfully and with such faith to the original that it seems to carry the patina of centuries. The old castle was destroyed in 1719, during the Jacobite Rising of that year, when English warships bombarded it, and then, after the surrender of its Spanish garrison, (who had no artillery to defend themselves), it was blown up. That was a great pity, for it was an ancient building, in parts 700 years old, and itself built on one of the vitrified forts still found up

EILEAN DONAN CASTLE

this west coast. But the restoration has been so well done that here, at least, we can sense more of the past than is possible in other similar castles of similar age, which are today in ruins. Castle Tioram in Moidart, and Mingary Castle in Ardnamurchan are much the same age as Eilean Donan, and they are ruins, lovely and evocative, but demanding much imagination to people them. Here, at Eilean Donan, history is a visible and palpable thing.

Rarely, before the day of its destruction, was Eilean Donan taken on by an enemy. One occasion was in 1715, when the castle had been taken over, peacefully, by the Government troops. The people of Kintail, of course, were Jacobite to a man, and the Hanoverian occupation of the castle was a very sore point. A local farmer approached the garrison commander and asked that the troops should come out and work in the fields to gather the harvest, for a storm was threatening. The gullible commander agreed, and when the troops returned, they found the castle occupied by the Jacobites, who were dancing with glee on the lead roof.

Like all old castles, its history is studded with a hundred legends, most of them bloody. In 1330, the castle was held by rebels against the King. Robert Bruce had died the year before and his great work in unifying the country was in danger. The Earl of Moray, nephew of Bruce, attacked the castle, defeated the garrison, and had all fifty of the rebels beheaded and their heads stuck on spikes around the walls. In 1529 the castle was attacked by the MacDonalds of Sleat, at a time when only 4 men of the Mackenzies were in the castle. One of those was killed immediately, but then MacDonald of Sleat was struck in the leg by an arrow. He was carried away to the little island of Glas Eilean nearby, and the attack continued without him. However, when the arrow was pulled out of the chief's leg, the barb severed an artery, and MacDonald died. His men then withdrew, carrying their dead chief.

Mackenzie of Kintail was given extra grants of land by the Government for that exploit (although he had not been there at the time), because MacDonald had long been a nuisance and a menace to all around him, being one of those Highland chiefs whose life consisted of little but constant raids and battles and whose greed made Highland history such a sorry tale of blood and pillage.

The restoration of Eilan Donan Castle was started and paid for by Lt. Col John Macrae-Gilstrap, and the work done by local men. It all started in 1912, and took 20 years to complete at a cost of a quarter of a million pounds. The restoration was done with love and care, and every detail, including many that can't be seen, was restored.

In the great Banqueting Hall, even the arrow-slits are there, small and unobtrusive, pointing inwards so that bowmen patrolling between the walls could keep an eye on all the guests and shoot them if necessary, a precaution hardly necessary even in the Highlands of the twentieth century.

During the restoration of the Castle, Miss Donaldson published her monumental book *Wanderings in the Western Highlands and Islands*, and in it she bitterly criticised the work being done, and the very idea of restoring a romantic and historic ruin. Miss Donaldson was a High Tory and a fervent Scottish nationalist, and if you think that this present book is somewhat bitter and prejudiced about the past, then you should read her, for she had a malign pen and was a mistress of invective. However, when the restoration was completed, she had to retract her attacks and admit that the results were splendid. If they pleased her, then without question they were acceptable and fitting to the Highlands she so loved.

Incidentally, the ladies who conduct visitors through the castle are very knowledgable and very much worth listening to.

The Mackenzies of Eilean Donan had always been loyal to the Stuart line, and were of course 'out' in 1745. Their title of the Earls of Seaforth was forfeited as a result, and not restored for 30 years. When it was restored, and the Earl returned to his lands, there was the problem of what to do with all the fighting men of Kintail who had followed him and his forebears so faithfully. There was no room any longer in the Highlands for private armies, nor was there need for them, for the Stuart cause had gone to final defeat and the land was peaceful.

So the Earl formed a regiment of his men, the Seaforths, to join the British Army, where the Highlanders' fighting qualities were respected and wanted. In 1778 a regiment was raised, mostly MacRaes of Kintail, and marched off to Leith on their way to India. However, in Edinburgh there was a strong rumour that the regiment had been sold to the East India Company, under terms of service much inferior to what the men had been promised. They mutinied and occupied Arthur's Seat in Edinburgh for several days, with great discipline and utter determination. Finally, they were persuaded that although indeed bound for India, it was as part of the British Army, and they boarded the ships at Leith.

It was a fateful journey, though, for scurvy and some other epidemic killed 250 men, including the Earl, and only 370 were left for service in India. A pity they had not stayed in the glens and straths of Kintail.

Just past Eilean Donan, at Dornie, a bridge carries you over the narrow neck of Loch Long down the shores of Loch Alsh and to Lochalsh itself. Just before the bridge a minor road runs up the east side of Loch Long to Bundalloch. It is a pleasant little side trip, and Bundalloch is a typical crofting village, not on the road to anywhere, and so comparatively unchanged.

Dornie itself was one of the many new villages established as a result of the clearances in Kintail, when the tenants were evicted from their holdings and resettled on the infertile sea shores. The public road ends there, but a track continues for some miles up Glen Elchaig towards the Falls of Glomach. The track goes much further in fact, winding on most delightfully past lochs and through passes to distant Loch Monar.

The good land around Loch Monar was once the summer shieling for all the people of Kintail, and that track was their route to it. The women and youngsters spent their summers there, grazing the animals on the sweet mountain grasses, making butter and cheese and keeping the animals away from the cultivated lowlands, where the men worked through the summer, growing the corn and other crops. It was this combination of lowland and upland grazing that made the Highlands so productive.

As soon as the farmers were deprived of their mountain grazings, agriculture ceased to be viable, the land suffered, and the people were pushed into deprivation and poverty. Those lands of Glen Elchaig suffered in that way, even during the days of the Earls of Seaforth, who, generally, were good proprietors.

There was a factor, Duncan Macrae, who had his own sheep farm, and he evicted many tenants from the Glen to add their land to his own. Particularly odious methods were used to force the tenants out, and many of them were forced to emigrate to Canada. As it happened, Macrae prospered for a while, but died in poverty.

Back at the main road (A87) there is Ardelve, today a pleasant village. It was here that the crofters from most of Lochalsh were settled in 1801 when the land was sold to Sir Hugh Innes.

Beyond again is Auchtertyre and Kirkton, which is the beginning of the National Trust for Scotland property in Lochalsh. Kirkton is an old crofting village, again with a sad history. In 1849 the crofters there were deprived of their summer grazing lands, and were reduced to swimming the cattle over to Skye for the summer.

Beyond the church there is the hill of Tulloch Ard. In time of trouble, a burning tar barrel at the top of that hill was the signal for Seaforth's fighting men to assemble at Eilean Donan.

LOCH ALSH, STROMEFERRY, LOCH CARRON, KISHORN, APPLECROSS, SHIELDAIG.

The National Trust for Scotland owns much of the Loch Alsh Peninsula. It was bequeathed to the Trust as long ago as 1946, and, true to its mandate, the Trust has protected this area from most of the 'development' horrors that have afflicted some parts of the Highlands.

Perhaps the show piece of Lochalsh is the Woodland Garden, on the Balmacara Estate. These are delightful at any time of the year, but, like most Highland gardens, are at their best in spring and early summer. Walks criss-cross through the woods and glades, and there is an astonishing variety of native trees, shrubs and plants, plus a grand interspersed collection of exotics from as far away as Tasmania, China and Chile. For anyone spending a holiday on the Lochalsh peninsula, happy days could pass wandering those woodland paths.

Because it is National Trust for Scotland property, there is a vast range of walks at Lochalsh, and they are well maintained and marked, although not obtrusively so. An enquiry at the Information Service or the NTS office will produce a wealth of booklets and leaflets to guide you on your way.

There is great pleasure in the walks. The wealth of wild flowers, the numbers of birds, the interesting traces of old lazy-bed and run-rig agriculture would alone make them memorable. And that is not to mention the views. Those views are strange and involved, and never less than beautiful. Hill and moor, fertile glen and green

Wholefood
Café & Restaurant

*Specializing in local seafood
and vegetarian dishes*

Highland Designworks
Plockton Road
Kyle of Lochalsh
Wester Ross IV40 8DA
Telephone 0599 4388

sea over white sand, heather and bracken in a thousand tweed-like shades, all combine in a wonderful tapestry that can never pall.

Kyle of Lochalsh itself, the ferry terminal for Skye, is not exactly an enthralling place, but it is always bustling and lively, and certainly is a very fine centre for exploring the countryside.

Kyle of Lochalsh, somewhat like Mallaig to the south, grew with the railway, and that only reached there in the 1890's. Until quite recently Lochalsh was not easy to get to, and throughout most of history it has been isolated, cut off by high mountains and the sea. Today it is accessible enough, but for most people it is just somewhere you pass through on the road to Skye. That is a pity, in a way, for it means that most people miss its unique beauties. On the other hand, it also means that those beauties are kept comparatively unspoiled and undeveloped.

It was here at Lochalsh that King Haco's fleet anchored on its way from Norway to Largs, where it was met and defeated by the ships of the Scottish king, a battle which changed the course of history and allowed the development of a Scottish State. The Norse fleet, it is recorded in Haco's Saga, anchored by the Carlin's Stone.

It was just by here, too, that one of the great heroes of

Fingalian legend drowned. The Fingalians were giants, of course, and one day they were happily running down deer on Skye, while their wives were at home on the mainland of Lochalsh. Their enemies took this opportunity of attacking and began burning the houses. The Fingalians saw the smoke rising, and rushed to the rescue, each of them leaping across the narrow Kyle of Lochalsh, using his spear as a vaulting pole. Unfortunately, though, the spear-shaft of Reidh snapped as he was jumping, and he fell into the sea and was drowned. He is immortalised in the name of *Kyle Rhea.*

At Balmacara Bay there is a cave where Prince Charles Edward stayed for a while after leaving Skye, and when he was a fugitive with an enormous price on his head. The cave is not easy to find even today, and you had best ask some local person for directions.

Carn Cloinn Mhic Cruimein is also there -- the Cairn of the Clan MacCrimmon. It marks the grave of the MacCrimmon men from Glenelg who long ago invaded Lochalsh. The men of Lochalsh, doughty warriors, drove them back, and above Kyle Rhea the MacCrimmons rested, believing themselves safe at last. They were far from safe, for the Mathesons of Lochalsh were close behind them, and as the MacCrimmons slept, the Mathesons came up and slaughtered them all. The Cairn marks the place.

There is a good new road (A890) running due north from Lochalsh to Strome Ferry, which allows you to bypass the Lochalsh peninsula if you wish. It would be a pity to do that, though, for the peninsula has its own particular charms. However, if you do take that road, you will pass the monument to Donald Murchison. It does not tell the story of how he collected the rents of these lands and smuggled them to the exiled Earl of Seaforth after the '19, nor of Seaforth's ingratitude for this, a story retailed in an earlier section of this book.

The road continues past a quite unobtrusive dam and loch, part of the Hydro schemes, and past the entrance to Gleann Udalain. There are no particular tracks, but it is good walking up the glen, following the burn. No people live in the glen these days, but 200 years ago that glen alone could muster 700 fighting men at the signal of the Mathesons of Loch Alsh.

North of Kyle of Lochalsh the other road, the one round the peninsula, runs together with the railway along the coast for some distance, and then the road takes off over the moors to Plockton.

Plockton is not part of the National Trust for Scotland property: it was bequeathed to the community by Lady Hamilton, who had gifted Balmacara Estate to the Trust.

A 'plock' is, unromantically, no more then a lump of land, and Plockton village lies indeed on a lump, a headland facing out to Loch Carron. It may not have a romantic name, but it is a fine village indeed, in a most romantic and lovely setting. There is even a row of palm trees along the shore!

Of course, these waters are a heaven for yachtsmen, and Plockton Bay in summer is a grand and gay sight. But you don't have to be a yachtsman to enjoy Plockton and the hinterland. It is magnificent walking country, both along the coast and over the inland moors, with a great wealth of mountain views.

The castle glimpsed through the trees across the bay from Plockton is Duncraig. It was built last century by Sir Alex. Matheson, but today is a school. He started building his castle in 1841, not long after he returned to the Highlands from the Far East. There he had worked in the great firm of merchants, Jardine Matheson, founded by his uncle, and had made a vast fortune. The unscrupulous methods by which that fortune was made do not bear close examination today, for that was the time of the Opium Wars in China, when the great British firms, and others, supported by their governments, fought for their 'right' to import Indian opium into China, against the will of the Chinese government.

However, by whatever means Alex. Matheson acquired great riches, he was a very reasonable Highland proprietor over all his vast estates. It was said that he could walk from the Atlantic to the North Sea without setting foot off his own land, and, to give him credit, he resisted all clearances on those estates. His successors, those who bought his estates towards the end of Matheson's life when his fortune was dwindling, had no such qualms, and the clearances here were as vicious as anywhere in the Highlands. Five hundred and thirty seven people were living in Plockton in the 1840's: today there is only half that number.

The road from Plockton to Strome Ferry is very fine, passing over grand open country and through steep bare hills. There is in particular one spectacular viewpoint where the road from Plockton meets the new road (A890) from Lochalsh. The whole lovely length of Loch Carron opens up under the road as it runs down to Strome Ferry.

There is sadness, though, in this delightful run, as well as great beauty, for everywhere are signs of deserted and derelict crofting land.

This is really the beginning of the harsher land that lies still further north. The underlying rocks here do not easily break down into fertile soil, and increasingly the landscape is one of bare, weathered rock, wild, windswept and empty.

There is no ferry now at Strome Ferry. There used to be one, not so long ago, and it was one of the notorious bottlenecks for traffic on its impatient way north. Today, a new road runs along the east side of Loch Carron, and that is the way north.

A hundred years ago, Strome Ferry figured largely in one of the most dramatic criminal cases of all time. A ship, the *S.S. Ferret*, registered at Strome Ferry, and based there, was stolen and later discovered in Australia. The *Ferret* was a sturdy vessel of 346 tons, designed to sail in the stormy waters of the Minch and round the Hebrides. In those days, the railway did not run on to Kyle of Lochalsh, but ended at Strome Ferry, and all the goods for the islands and much of the west coast came by rail to Strome Ferry and were then transhipped to vesels such as the *Ferret*.

But *Ferret* disappeared one day in 1880, and was not located (indeed, she was feared lost at sea) until June of 1881, when it was announced that she had been seen, and arrested, at Melbourne in far-away Australia.

She was actually spotted by a Glasgow policeman who had emigrated to Australia. He knew the ship, had seen her often in the Clyde, and had been disturbed by reading reports of her loss in the Glasgow papers, which, as in so many cases, were sent to him by his family at home.

When police boarded her, they uncovered a strange story indeed. They found forged ship's papers, a code book for messages to some mysterious agent in London, which contained sinister codes for such things as disposing of the crew, and even a printing press for producing forged bills of lading. It was discovered that *Ferret* had been stolen in the Clyde, sailed to Cardiff for coaling, then went off south to Gibraltar, entered the Mediterranean, then doubled back, undetected of course in those days, and crossed the Atlantic to Brazil. There she picked up a cargo of coffee for Capetown, but on that long ocean crossing ran out of coal, and some of the coffee beans were burned in the boilers to keep her moving. The remains of the cargo were profitable, though, and fetched £10,000 in Capetown.

A certain Henderson, who claimed to be the owner of the vessel, cabled £8,000 of this to the mysterious London Agent, and *Ferret* sailed in ballast to Melbourne, where Henderson tried to sell the ship.

Thanks to the ex-Glasgow policeman, the plot was foiled. Henderson, the captain and the purser went to jail for seven years, but it was never discovered who was the London agent. He was obviously the brains and the moving spirit of the whole enterprise, and he escaped scot-free.

As for *S.S. Ferret,* she stayed in Australia, and sailed those coasts until 1920, when she was finally wrecked in a storm.

The road along the east coast of Loch Carron, which has replaced the ferry, was certainly not an easy road to build. The rock faces above it are split and rotten in many places. Great steel nets have had to be installed to stop rocks slips, but even so the signs which warn you to 'Beware of fallen rocks' are not be be disregarded.

It is a pleasant road, looking out over the loch and with distant views of the Applecross mountains. Perhaps it lacks the grandeur of some Highland roads, but, as ever, there are wondrous light effects on the water and the hills.

At the head of the loch, the road from Achnasheen comes in from the north-east. That road, the A890, runs the length of Glen Carron, as does the railway. Like other glens going west to east, Glen Carron has throughout all of history been used as a highway.

Travelling that road to Achnasheen is a vivid example of the difference between a Highland strath and a Highland glen. A strath is a wide fertile valley, while a glen may be no more than a cleft between mountains. At first the road to Achnasheen goes up a 'strath', where the river Carron runs from the delightful Loch Dughaill. Then, around Craig, the valley sides pinch together into what is most certainly a glen, and a grand one.

Much of this land is now owned by the Forestry Commission, and is under the inevitable conifers, but there are high hills in the background, and splendid panoramas of the distant heights.

It was on those bare hills, the shoulder of Fuar Tholl, that the Prince of Wales, later Edward VII, almost met an untimely death. He and his companions were enjoying the very questionable delights of a deer hunt (hunt, not stalk, for the deer were driven up to the guns) when a great rock fall thundered down from the heights above, very narrowly missing the Prince. It was almost as though a message was coming from on high. It did not spoil their sport, though, for they bagged nineteen stags that day.

A very fine track runs off northward from the A890 just west of Craig, behind Achnashelach railway station. It runs through forestry plantations, then follows the river Lair, foaming through narrow gorges and then over the Coulin pass by Loch Coulin and Loch Clair. The views across the lochs to Glen Torridon, with the quartzite summits of Beinn Eighe and Liathach shining white, are fine indeed. The track eventually joins the A896 Kinlochewe to Torridon road. It is very much a track for walking, not driving, even if vehicles were permitted. It is a right of way, though, and was established as such by a legal battle in the 1930's. Originally it was a road cut for the convenience of the proprietor of Coulin Lodge, so that he had easy access to the railway in Glen Carron. Now it is an excellent and not too strenuous walk through very lonely country, with Carn Breac on one side and Beinn Liath Mhor on the other.

If the walkers are dropped at Craig, the driver can enjoy the trip up to Achnasheen, lunch leisurely there perhaps, then drive on through Glen Docherty to Kinlochewe and pick up the walkers by Loch Clair. It is hard to imagine a more satisfying day for walkers and driver.

There is not a great deal to Achnasheen itself, although it is an attractive village. But it is a very important road junction, and very central for touring the Highlands. Glen Docherty, Strath Bran and Glen Carron all join there, and as well as having been means of communication from time immemorial, they all have their particular delights and character. In particular, perhaps, although it is difficult to make such a choice, the road to the west through Glen Docherty is one not to be missed. Indeed, when visiting the Highlands, such choices have to be made constantly. There never is enough time for everything that should be done, and inevitably something has to be scrimped or missed. A lifetime would not be long enough to sample all the delights available: to choose between them is as difficult as any judgement that Paris ever had to make.

The road (A832) to Kinlochewe runs first along the quite charming length of Loch a' Chroisg, then sweeps upwards very satisfyingly to a spectacular view near Lubmore, where all the grandeur of the Coulin Forest with its stark moorlands and bare peaks are spread out below you, and then sweeps down through Glen Docherty to Kinlochewe. If, though, you are keeping to the west from Loch Carron, then you will turn left where the road from Strome Ferry joins the road to Achnasheen, and will be on A896 for

Lochcarron.

In the old days, before the ferry at Strome Ferry was replaced by the new road up the east side of Loch Carron, there was a major road down the west side of the loch to the ferry slip near Strome Castle. A major road once, it is now a very a quiet side road, leading only to the castle and a little beyond, but is well worth taking, even if it is another deadend.

There is not much left of Strome Castle today, which is one of the few total ruins owned by the National Trust for Scotland, and they have, surely wisely, left it to moulder away in peace. It was an ancient castle of the Macdonnels of Glengarry, whose main territory was away south in Knoydart.

It had long been something of an irritant to the Mackenzies of Kintail, who were constantly seeking greater influence and more land in the west. In 1602, after a century of bloody feuding, the Mackenzies mounted a determined siege of the castle, but the Macdonnels were equally determined, and it was indeed a strong castle. Eventually the Mackenzies were on the point of giving up and going home when a Mackenzie who had been a prisoner in the castle jumped off the parapet (permanently injuring himself in doing so) and told the besieging forces that the Macdonnels were in trouble because the supply of gun powder was exhausted. The Mackenzies made one last great effort, and captured the castle.

Then the story became known. In fact, there was an ample supply of gunpowder in the castle, but it had been sabotaged by some women of the Mackenzies, held prisoner in the castle, who had managed to soak the barrels of powder and make it useless. It is said that it was the task of the Mackenzie women to draw water from the well, and they had managed to pour water into the barrels of gunpowder. Another story is that the women used a different, more earthy but no less effective way of soaking the powder. Whatever method they used, it worked, and the Mackenzies took Strome Castle and destroyed it, and thus ended the Macdonnels territorial ambitions round Loch Carron.

If you have travelled the length of this quiet road to Strome Castle, then do go on a little further, to the end of the road, at Ardnaneaskan. There is nothing there but scenery, but it is truly magnificent. There are remains of the old hardwood forests as well as views of great mountains across the waters of Loch Kishorn. The mouth of Loch Carron is bestrewn with islands, and it is lovely almost beyond words.

There are very obvious raised beaches along both sides of Loch Carron, at 25 and 50 feet above the loch. At Strome Ferry there is also a beach at 100 feet. These look like old roads running perfectly level, hugging every bend and headland of the loch, but in fact they mark the various water levels reached by the loch in ancient days when glaciers and the melt water from glaciers were forming the pattern of all the west coast.

Of course, you have to go back to Lochcarron, and there the road swings across the neck of the land to Kishorn and Loch Kishorn.

A hundred and fifty years ago, Kishorn became known nationally because of the Kishorn dwarfs. Those little people, two brothers and a sister, had been born to parents of normal stature, but the children were no more than 45 inches tall. They were found by some company of travelling players and taken to London. They even performed before the Queen, dressed in Mackenzie tartan and singing

Gaelic songs. She, with her besotted love of everything Highland, must have found them at least amusing. Their performance was said to be "superior to that of Tom Thumb exhibited by Barnum." There is a memorial stone to those little people in the old churchyard at Lochcarron.

But there is a lot more to Kishorn than a history of exploited dwarfism. For one thing, the views across the loch and over to the great barrier of the Applecross mountains. For another, there are interesting National Nature Reserves here, where the natural plants and trees of north-west Scotland are allowed to grow and reproduce, as they did some hundreds of years ago.

The Rossal Ashwood, flourishing on the limestone soil and surrounded by undisturbed grassland rich with wild flowers, is well worth a visit at any time, but perhaps especially in spring, when the flowers are in full glory and the trees in fresh leaf.

The Allt nan Carnan Gorge has a wide variety of Scottish plant life -- oak, birch, pine, elm and gean (cherry) growing in a gorge in places 80 feet deep. A fine, secretive place.

Beyond Kishorn the road swings north, either direct to Shieldaig or forking west again to the remote and desolate Applecross peninsula. Surely few people will have come so far and not wish to visit Applecross, the more so now that there is a circular route. Before you take the Applecross road, you will be confronted with one of the few industrial complexes in this part of Scotland. It is a great construction plant for North Sea Oil Rigs, and it is, perhaps inescapably, ugly. It was not put there without a great battle, and without asurances that it would not be allowed to damage the society in which it was placed. Of course, it did, gravely, and it is difficult to know what benefits the local people have received from it. One can but hope that when it is no longer required, when the oil runs out, that plant will be removed, and Loch Kishorn allowed to regain its former glory. One may hope for that, but doubt it.

To reach Applecross, you must face the notorious Beallach na Ba, the Pass of the Cattle. Don't, though, be unduly alarmed. It is a steep and narrow and twisting road, but a reasonable vehicle and reasonable care, as well as a reasonable road surface these days, has robbed it of most terrors. In summer, that is: it is a very different story on a night of January storm.

The pass climbs to a summit of 2100 feet in six miles direct from sea level, and the views, for the passengers, are grand and dramatic. There is one point, near the summit, where the view back down to Loch Kishorn is framed by two great symmetrical bare hills, with the loch far below. It is so dramatic a view that it appears to have been staged, and you almost expect footlights and an orchestra bursting into a great Wagnerian overture.

There is a small plateau at the top of the pass, barren and rockstrewn. Most people, very reasonably, stop there to survey the scene, and it is simply splendid. Mountain, moors, lochs in every direction and in every shape. The air blows keen and fresh there, and with the subtle tang of salt and seaweed and heather. Indeed a view to savour.

Don't be misled by the many cairns on that hilltop. They have no significance: they are not funeral cairns built by those who bore their dead from afar and built cairns where they rested. These are no more than toys put up by casual visitors, intent on changing the scenery they have come so far to enjoy. Ignore, too, if you can, the detritus of chocolate wrappers, crisp packets and beer cans which *homo touristica* seems to find essential to his well-being.

The road from the top of the pass down to Applecross is much less dramatic than the climb up, but nevertheless has its own beauties. It is stark moorland, wild and desolate, and inhospitable, marked here and there by peat diggings, which are worked every year by the local people. You don't see very much of that these days, which is a great shame, but here you can see it, and understand the amount of labour which goes into the domestic production of the fragrant peat blocks. It may be free fuel, but there is a great cost in labour.

Applecross is a strange name to find in the remote north-west of Scotland, perhaps more reminiscent of Hereford or Somerset than of these bleak hills. It is a corruption, an Anglicising, of the Gaelic, of course, and was once, long ago, *Aper-Crossan*, the mouth or estuary of the Crossan river. But 'Applecross' itself is an ancient name, and has been found on documents dating back to 1275. It is easy to see how 'Aper-Crossan' became 'Applecross'. But it has nothing to do with apples! The name merely perpetuates the simple mistake made one day by some tired monk as he copied parchments.

The settlement goes back to St. Maol Rubha, who, next to Calum Cille himself, was the most celebrated and successful missionary of the early Christian church in the north. He was born in 641 at Bangor in Ireland, and crossed to Scotland in 671. He established his church there at Applecross, and maintained it, as Abbot, for 51 years.

Maol Rubha did not spend all his days at Applecross, but travelled widely over the north of Scotland, carrying his beliefs to many and far-distant places. In 722 he fell mortally ill when proselytising in the distant Black Isle, near Inverness. Knowing that he was dying, he asked that his body be taken back to Applecross for burial. His new converts in the Black Isle, though, thought to bury him there. They tried, and tried repeatedly, but found they could not move the saint's body to the newly-dug grave. Eventually they sent a message to Applecross, and four men came from there (legend says they were all red-headed -- the saint was himself red-headed), effortlessly lifted the saint and carried him back to Applecross for burial, resting only once on their long journey. So St. Maol Rubha lies today in Applecross, as he wished, although we know not where he lies. Probably, though he is buried in what is still known as the Saint's Grave, which is marked by two large rounded stones, lying east and west.

That has long been a sacred place, and there was was once an ancient belief that a traveller from Applecross, or a soldier going to battle, should carry a pinch of soil from there, and thus would be guaranteed a safe return.

Like several other places in Scotland, the area around Applecross was declared a Christian sanctuary. Indeed, a very ancient name for the area was A' Chomraidh, which simply means 'Sanctuary', and it continued to be a Sanctuary until the Reformation. Any fugitive reaching there was safe from secular justice -- and justice could be hellish rough in the old days of the clans. Because it was a Christian sanctuary, it was also protected from the incessant warfare which wrent and wracked, and almost ruined, the Highlands.

Only once was the sanctuary violated, when one day the savage Norsemen appeared out of the west, and indulged in their normal burning, rape and robbery. As they rowed away, leaving destruction behind them, their ships inexplicably sank in a calm sea and a light wind.

A very interesting and ancient custom persisted in Applecross at least up to the middle of the 17th century. Bulls were sacrificed on August 27th, the saint's day of Maol Rubha. Bulls and the sacrifice of them were probably an important part of the religion of the ancient Picts, of whom almost nothing is known except what can be inferred from their remarkable and lovely carved stones. Those stones often carry the effigies of bulls, and it is interesting to ponder about possible connections between the Picts and the old Mithraic religion where bulls were also worshipped and sacrificed, and which, even in the heyday of the Roman Empire, was as powerful as Christianity.

This was traditionally Mackenzie country, and difficult though it is to believe today, was once productive and well populated. In 1792, three thousand black cattle from the Applecross peninsula were walked over Bealleach na Ba (the name means Pass of the Cattle) on their way south.

In the 1860's Lord Middleton bought the property from the Duke of Leeds, who had bought it from the Mackenzie chief (who had no right to sell it, in the first place). Middleton very ruthlessly cleared all the land of its people and their cattle, and left it for the deer, which it was his delight to shoot.

Applecross village today is still tiny and quiet, with a delightful setting in a deep bay of red sand -- red because the red sandstone mountains of Torridon are nearby. Even on your first visit to Applecross you might think it strangely familiar, that is, if you have a long memory and are a cinema goer. It was here that the excellent comedy *Laxford Hall* was made back in the 1950's, a film not only extremely funny, but very true to Highland life. The classic chase of the poachers was over Beallach na Ba, and that was in the days before the road was tarmacadamed.

The approach to the village, once having left the bareness of the Beallach, is through a green and pleasant glen, a surprising contrast after the bleakness of the Pass. It was in the glen that most of the population lived until they were cleared off to the coast lest they interfere with the deer kept for the proprietor's pleasures and profit. In 1836, three thousand people lived in Applecross parish, most of them in this glen.

The old road swings south from the village, hugging the coast at first and then cutting across a narrow neck of land to Loch Toscaig and Toscaig village. The road ends there. The loch is a fine narrow sea loch, and the views grand, with the Crowlin Islands scattered over the sea, and with Raasay, Scalpay and Lunga islands. Skye broods in the background, with Glamaig and Beinn Dearg and in the distance the great Cuillins. It is very much worth while travelling this lonely road for such a sight at the end.

There used to be a well-trodden footpath from Toscaig back across country to Russel on Loch Kishorn. It is not well-trodden these days, but can still be traced, and makes a fine piece of Highland tramping.

Today there is a new road out of Applecross, northward round the peninsula to Shieldaig. Before that road was carved there were only precarious foot-tracks joining the tiny communities to the metropolis of Applecross village or Shieldaig. Naturally there was a steady depopulation, and in the 1960's the local authority suggested evacuating all the people from those coastal communities and re-settling them elsewhere. Not surprisingly, these was a great outcry of indignation, for anything smacking of further clearances touches very raw nerves indeed in the Highlands -- for that matter in all of Scotland.

So in 1965 the road was started, driving slowly down from Shieldaig. It is a road that could not have made much sense economically, but there is more to life than the bottom figures on a balance sheet. This new road has greatly reduced the isolation of Applecross and the other villages, for that road has no high pass to climb and, being by the coast, is rarely affected by snow.

Before that road was built, the people of Applecross were much more isolated than had they lived on a small island. Their only sure communication was by the MacBraynes steamer which lay off-shore and transhipped goods and passengers to rowing boats from the village. Since that was usually done at 3 a.m., it was not exactly easy. Then there was a ferry started from Toscaig to Kyle of Lochalsh, but the boat was neither reliable nor safe, and there was general relief when she was retired with the opening of the new road.

Staying close to the coast, the road opens up completely new country to the visitor. There are a few scattered houses and crofts along the road, but nothing in the way of a real village, only scenery, hills and moors, lochs and distant islands, and a sea that can be coloured like some great enamelled bowl.

The road runs right to the northern tip of the Applecross Peninsula, and then leaves the waters of the Inner Sound and swings south-east to run down Loch Torridon to Shieldaig.

There is another road from the south to Shieldaig, and of course that is the one you would take if you did not want to face the Bealleach Na Ba and the long road north round the Applecross Peninsula. That road, (A896), runs due north from Kishorn across the neck of the Peninsula. It is a grand quiet road, with hardly a house along its length, but with plenty of interest on both sides. There is a very special viewpoint there, about a mile north of where the road touches Loch Coultrie. You can see all the starkness of

Applecross from there, with the moors speckled with tiny lochans and the slopes of An Staonach and Beinn Bhan. In the other direction, there is Loch Coultrie and Loch Damh and behind them the emptiness of hills and mountains running to distant Achnasheen.

Shieldaig, at the head of Loch Shieldaig, itself emptying into Loch Torridon, gets its Gaelic name from a much older Norse name, *Sild-vik*, or Herring Bay. This indicates for how many centuries the herring shoaled in their countless thousands up these coasts. They don't do that now, though.

Shieldaig is a place unique in the Highlands. This village on the coast was not started and built by the dispossessed crofters from the surrounding glens, as were most coastal villages. Nor was it built as a railhead or as a fishing community. Instead, it was built specifically to provide sailors for the Royal Navy.

In Napoleonic times, French war-ships were constantly active round these waters, making quick raids here and there, and harrying the coastal shipping and generally being an expensive nuisance and occupying the attention of British ships which would have been better employed blockading and harrying the French coasts. The Duke of Argyll had the answer. British ships, he argued, were much too precious to be entrusted to the scum of the English towns, the tailors and shoemakers pressed into service. The best sailors for manning British ships were to be found on the west and north coasts of Scotland, from Galloway to the Orkneys, and it was there that they should be encouraged. The Highland proprietors, though, he went on, were reluctant to give land for communities where such Jolly Jack Tars could be reared and trained. (There is no record of the Duke offering any of his lands for that purpose.) Therefore the King and his Lords in Council should set up a village at Shieldaig for bringing youths to a knowledge of the sea.

As it happened, there was already a considerable community of quite prosperous cattle farmers at Shieldaig, and they were not very enthusiastic about the proposal. Indeed, it took ten years before a consortium of businessmen undertook to build the village, helped by

TIGH AN EILEAN HOTEL
Shieldaig, Ross-shire. IV54 8XN.
This small centrally-heated hotel of 12 rooms is on the shore of Loch Torridon, amongst some of the most spectacular scenery in Wester Ross.
It is an ideal touring centre, with the Applecross peninsula and the Beinn Eighe Nature Reserve nearby.
Boat hire, hill walking, bird watching and fishing are all here, and all these activities, and the very comfortable, fully licensed hotel with its excellent food ensure a momentous stay for young and old alike.
Tel: 05205 251.   Fax. 05205 321.

the Government, which provided facilities -- rather like the various grants sometimes available today. Boat building was encouraged and developed, a system of guaranteed prices for fish introduced, land grants made, and tax-free salt provided -- a very important provision in those days of salt herring and a Government salt monopoly. The government even built a new road between Kishorn and Shieldaig. It was all a bit like most of the government activities we hear about today: the remedy is only applied when the illness is over.

By the time the new village was functioning, Napoleon and the threat he represented had slipped into history, and there is no record of how many sailors from Shieldaig joined the Royal Navy, which by that time was much reduced anyway.

Then the Mackenzies sold the land to the Duke of Leeds. The Duchess, who was of the same family responsible for the ruthless Sutherland Clearances, cared nothing for special government tenancies or special tenant rights in the government village. She wanted it cleared; she wanted sheep, not mariners. And she got them, by the usual ruthless methods. The perpetual tenancies granted by the government in London were ignored, and the people driven away from the land on which they relied. Forced to depend entirely on the uncertain fishing, they quickly sank into a desperate poverty, and by the time the estate was sold to Sir John Stewart, only one boat was working off-shore from Shieldaig.

Stewart, in spite of his name, was no less ruthless than the Duchess, and he intensified the clearances, and made a desolation out of what had once long been prosperity.

But it is all in the past now, and Shieldaig is a quiet place, superbly situated on Loch Shieldaig and with the sublimity of Ben Shieldaig close by, with all its shelving precipices, wooded gullies and ledges.

Today the village is not actually on the main road -- there is a bypass. Unless you are in the greatest of hurries, though, the short circuit into the village itself is well worth making, even if only to enjoy its magnificent situation.

Then, just after the junction as you leave the village and rejoin the main road to Torridon, there is one of the grandest views of loch and mountain to be found anywhere in this land of loch and mountain. Stop at the parking place and savour it. Upper Loch Torridon is spread out before you, and Loch Shieldaig and the high mountains across the loch: Beinn Alligan, Beinn Dearg, Beinn Bhreac. It is a scene of unblemished loveliness, and one to be cherished and long remembered. Below you is the old road, now a foot track, and a fine one.

TORRIDON, DIABEG,, KINLOCHEWE, LOCH MAREE, GAIRLOCH, INVEREWE, LOCH BROOM, ULLAPOOL

From Shieldaig the road (A896) travels along the southern side of Upper Loch Torridon to Torridon. It is a good road, and gives excellent viewing of the loch and of the Ben-Damph Forest.

Torridon really is the introduction to the Torridon Highlands and the ancient rocks of that strange and geologically twisted landscape. The red sandstone of Torridon is one of the oldest rocks in the world, having been laid down perhaps 750 million years ago. In places it is capped by a hard white quartzite, and some of the peaks gleam white, seeming snow-sprinkled even in summer.

Not surprisingly, there is a sense of great age in these mountains, which have been little changed and manipulated by man, as has so much of our countryside. What we see is what nature alone has made, and nature has made something weird and primeval, where the mountains rise like great prehistoric monsters from treeless rock, and where every hollow holds its own tiny lochan, with a floor of solid rock. It as almost as though the Act of Creation has been halted, and nature is waiting for it to be resumed.

Perhaps the most weird and most wild is Liathach, the Grey One, which towers white-capped above Torridon village -- a great treacherous, crumbling pile with pinnacles remote and distant. A strange mountain, haunted almost, and one not to be braved except by the skilled and well-equipped.

To best appreciate Loch Torridon, visit the north side. Keep left at Torridon village, coming from Shieldaig, and travel that minor road over the Pass of the Winds to Diabaig. This is a road that Queen Victoria enjoyed when she travelled it in September 1877. She was staying at Loch Maree on one of her Highland jaunts. Accompanied by the inevitable John Brown, amongst others, she found this a fine and wild uncivilised spot, like the end of the world, as she wrote in her diary, and she noted that 'hardly anyone ever comes here.' That last remark at least is still relatively quite true.

That road leads only to isolated houses and small villages, and is a dead-end road, but it surely is one of the most attractive little excursions on the west coast.

Like many such roads hereabouts, it has its residual sadness as well as its great beauty. There were some particularly heartless clearances in these glens, especially when the estate was sold in 1831 to a certain Col. McBarnet, a wealthy plantation owner from the West Indies -- so you can imagine how he acquired his wealth. The tenant farmers were immediately cleared off to allow sheep farming, and were left with only a scrap of ground to grow potatoes. McBarnet and his factor ruled that no tenant could keep any sheep or cattle, and the only cow was kept at the inn. Finally, in 1859, all the people were resettled at Annat, at the head of the loch, on land taken from the already miserably small holdings of the people there, land which was already exhausted and liable to flooding.

For once, there was a happier ending to the story. The estate was later sold to Duncan Darroch, a wealthy man from Gourock, near Glasgow, and a man with some local ancestry. Darroch wanted a deer forest, not a sheep farm, and he saw no conflict between crofters and deer. He believed, rightly, that sheep ruined the mountain grazings for deer as well as cattle. So he cleared off the sheep, restored the lower grazings to the crofters and allowed their cattle to share the hill grazings with the deer, a perfectly sensible and ecologically sound use of the land. He gave land to previously evicted tenants at Torridon, and that was the origin of the village we see there today. Moreover, he fenced off the crofting land so that the deer could not raid the growing crops, and he allowed timber to be cut for fencing and repairs. He allocated peat bogs for the old and new villages, and positively encouraged, instead of forbidding, the collection of seaweed for fertiliser. He insisted that no crofter keep sheep, but was very willing to lend money for the purchase of cattle or for building boats. That exemplary Highland proprietor lived on his estate and made it prosper, but the path he trod was not followed by others, whether Highland, Lowland, English or American.

Duncan Darroch died at Torridon House, and his tenants, without being asked, carried his body from Torridon all the way to distant Gourock for burial in the family vault.

There is a stone by the roadside just beyond Torridon, put there by Duncan's widow, Ann. It is:

'*In memory of the devotion and affection shown by one hundred men on the estate of Torridon, who, at their own request, carried his body from the house here on its way to interment in the family burial place at Gourock.*'

Perhaps it needs a Highlander to appreciate the subtle nuance of that act by the Torridon men. What they did was in fact the final act of homage to a dead chief. Nothing could have shown deeper respect.

Back, then, to the road along the north side of Upper Loch Torridon. There is a bridge just past the entrance to Torridon House, itself out of sight up the valley. You won't see it from your car, but that bridge crosses a great ravine cut deep in the rock by the river pouring down the cleft between Beinn Alligan and Liathach. It is a magnificent sight, with a fine waterfall at the northern end of the great stone trough, and well worth a long look.

A footpath begins just by the bridge, signposted by the National Trust for Scotland, which owns this land, and that path provides a walk of rare delight up the valley betwen Beinn Dearg and Liathach. From there, it passes between Liathach and Beinn Eighe and down into Glen Torridon by the Great Black Corries and eventually regains the road in the glen. It is not too strenuous, although as ever you must be properly equipped and careful in these hills, and it will give you a day of great delight in those empty places. You can in fact extend that walk if you take an unmarked but quite clear stalkers' track from the eastern side of Beinn Eighe. That track leads to the even more lonely and spectacular Coir Mhic Fhearchair.

The villages along this little road to Diabaig are amongst the most attractive on the whole west coast, and one can well understand why they are so popular with people retiring and seeking a peaceful seclusion. Much of the countryside is National Trust for Scotland property, and the Trust is concerned to maintain its beauty and character. That means, though, that little can change, and there is no opportunity for enterprise. It is not easy to make a living of any kind in that remote place: the pension cheque and the DHSS Giro are the main sources of income.

Alligin, that finely situated little village, suffered badly at the time of MacBarnet. It had been a reasonably prosperous little place, with each croft having 15 sheep and half a dozen cows, plus of course the proceeds from some fishing. MacBarnet's factor proposed that they give up their sheep, and the estate would rent the grazings from them for £50 a year. That seemed like a reasonable bargain, and it was agreed, but the estate paid the rent for only one year.

But affairs went from bad to very much worse, for then the crofters were deprived of their hill grazing and limited to keeping only one cow and its calf to six months. After that, they were deprived of a quarter of their arable land, which was given to the incoming shepherds. Thus their only source of income came from a bit of fish and the sale of one calf a year. They still struggled on, until relieved by the more kindly regime of Duncan Darroch, and the history of no part of the Highlands better illustrates the tenacity with which the Highland crofter stuck to the land and the way of life which had served his ancestors so well.

The end of the road comes at Lower Diabaig, a splendid little village with a superb situation. It lies in an arc of steep ground running down to little Loch Diabaig, and unusually for this coast, has a good beach. The stretch of road from Alligin to Diabaig forces its way through wild country, marked by great rough boulders.

The present road, which is certainly steep enough in places, does not follow the old track, which can be seen here and there up and down the hillside. This is Bealach na Gaoithe, The Pass of the Winds, and if you face a gale from the west there you will understand where the name came from.

Through the pass and you come to Loch Diabaigs Airde and from the western end of that little loch there is a fine view of the great ravine by which Loch Diabaigs Airde empties into the sea at Loch Diabaig, which is no more than a small inlet off Loch Torridon. Just by there you catch the first startling glimpse of the great steep natural amphitheatre where Diabaig lies, and it is not a sight soon forgotten.

For a walker, one of Scotland's best tracks carries on from Diabaig round the empty coast to Red Point ten miles or so north, which is the end of the road (B8056) from Gairloch. It is not a track with the mountain glories of others in this empty land, but it has its own very special glories of sea and sky and distant mountains. And quietness. And the smell of tangle and heather. Quite delectable on an autumn day of driving cloud and patchy sun.

From Diabaig, of course, you must drive back to Torridon, but as so often when you retrace your steps on these Highland roads, the return journey is just as enchanting as the outward journey, and the scenery, from a different point of view, just as refreshing. Reflect that had you been travelling this track a few generations ago, you would have been well refreshed with whisky on which no duty had ever been paid, for this was a famous place for distilling in the old days. It is not surprising, really that the Customs and Excise men -- the despised 'gaugers' made little progress in their kill-joy task here. There was no chance of them catching anyone by surprise, and there is an infinity of places to hide the still. These days, you will have to content yourself with a can of something from the village shop, a can of coke, perhaps, or better, a bottle of Scotland's own Irn Bru, a concoction which is, they claim, made from girders!

This land north of Loch Torridon was traditionally Mackenzie country. One of its most famous lairds was John Mackenzie, the 3rd laird, who was 'out', very gallantly, in the Uprising of 1745. He was a particularly handsome young man, and very popular with, and active amongst, the Jacobite ladies of Scotland, so popular and active indeed that he became a kind of pin-up for them. Later, after Culloden, when John Mackenzie was a fugitive and roaming the country with a price on his head, it was said that even if they captured him, the government would never dare to hang him, because if they did, half the ladies in Scotland would hang themselves in despair!

Beyond Torridon village, the road -- still A896 -- swings away north-east through Glen Torridon, under the shoulder of Beinn Eighe. Majestic though Beinn Eighe and its mightier neighbour Liathach are when seen from the road, these two great sisters turn their greatest beauties to the north, where the car-bound traveller cannot see them, and they are reserved for those who penetrate the passes on foot.

This is especially true of the vast Coire Mhic Fhearchair, a great horseshoe of 1000 foot slopes tumbling down to a lochan. This is a sight of loneliness and savage beauty almost unparalleled in these empty lands, but you can, fortunately, only reach it by foot and with some effort. A swim in the lochan is a reward for the effort of getting there, and you will find that the bottom is made up of firm rock slabs of green and red rock. Don't linger with your swim, though, for those waters feel like new-melted ice even on the hottest of days.

Much of the land to the north of the road is a National Nature Reserve. It was the first such reserve in Britain, and was established in 1951. It spreads from the end of Glen Torridon round the shoulder of Beinn Eighe and along the western side of Loch Maree. There are more than 10,000 acres of it, and within very wide limits, it is open to walking and exploration.

This road through Glen Torridon is always full of interest, and it swoops up and down very satisfyingly. The views to the south, just after the watershed, are particularly fine, with a grand chain of lochs running off to the distance. There has been much planting of the monotonous conifers in recent years, though, and as ever, some of the best panoramas are now blanketed by their dullness.

If you did not walk the track already recommended, from Achnashellach to this road, do at least stop now and walk the three miles or so to the head of Loch Coulin, using the obvious track. The views back over the road to Beinne Eighe are quite wonderful.

Kinlochewe village is at the junction of two roads, that from Torridon and the other from Achnasheen. Travelling from Torridon, and going on north, by the road up Loch Maree, you will have missed a glorious sight, and it is worth going a mile or two along the Achnasheen road up Glen Docherty to see it. There is an obvious view point there, and from it the view down the Glen to Loch Maree is one of sublime beauty. But it is not only Loch Maree, lying there silver under the great hills -- those hills are, always, clad in the softest of colours -- for the loch has a richness of islands, and it carries your eyes down its length to the distant sea. Near at hand Slioch rises steep from the valley, as shapely and almost unreal as a child's drawing of a mountain. There are the pink sandstone slopes of Meall a' Ghiubhais leading up to the corries of Beinn Eighe, wild and white. A scene, indeed, of wild magnificence, and the scatter of houses which are Kinlochewe does nothing to detract from its grandeur.

Kinlochewe itself is not a place of any great character or history. The name 'Kinlochewe ' is rather surprising, for it lies at the head of Loch Maree, not Loch Ewe, and should properly be Kinlochmaree. Of course long ago Loch Ewe and Loch Maree were one, with Loch Maree becoming separated as detritus from glaciers made the barrier between the two.

HIGHLAND CATTLE

KIRSTY

The main advantage of Kinlochewe, and it is a considerable one, is as a centre for exploring the almost infinite beauties of Loch Maree and the hills and glens around the loch. Vast areas of this land are owned by the National Trust for Scotland, and the Beinn Eighe National Nature Reserve, and thus are not only open to exploration, but are positively geared to it. More than that, though, these hills have a wonderful variety of flora and fauna, and provide opportunities for enjoying them, and such opportunities are increasingly scarce in Scotland today.

One of the most spectacular and obvious features of these great hills is their strange geology. They are capped with gleaming white quartzite, about 600 million years old, and that white cap rests on red Torridonian sandstone, laid down 750 million years ago, and they both in turn rest on beds of Lewisian gneiss which dates from perhaps 2000 million years ago. This complexity has been twisted and disrupted by earth movements over the aeons of time, and eroded by glaciers and carved by wind and rain and frost. Not surprisingly, the whole area is constantly quartered by geologists and their students.

And it is not only geologists who find these hills rewarding. Botanists, too, make pilgrimages here. There are lovely natural rock gardens growing on the sandstone shelves on these cliffs, and you certainly don't need to be a botanist to appreciate the beauties of those natural decorations.

That is the geology and the flora, but the fauna are there too, thriving in the security of the Reserves. There are red deer, of course, so that many that regular culling is necessary, and at the other end of the scale, the lovely little Pygmy Shrew. There are wild cats and foxes and pine martens, and the martens, which are rarely sighted elsewhere, have learned to haunt picnic sites for handouts. As for birds, there are golden eagles, but not so many, for each pair needs about 15,000 acres in which to forage. There are peregrine and merlin, ravens and a whole host of other unusual species.

So altogether, for anyone who appreciates or wants to learn

more about Scotland's wealth of flora and fauna, the Loch Maree area is virtually an essential. You will find lots of information to hand there, from the NTS and the Nature Conservancy Council, and knowledgeable people to send you off into the hills, along the Nature Trails and other tracks.

It is always wise to call at the Aultry Visitor Centre, about a mile west of Kinlochewe, before starting expeditions into these hills. Not only will you get the very latest information on sightings of birds and beasts, but will receive warnings of any particular problems. The exhibitions are always interesting. There is a convenient car park about a mile further along the road, and two of the nature trails start from there.

Perhaps the most evocative place to visit, if time does not permit more, is Coille na Glas Leitire, the Wood on the Grey Slopes. This is a remnant of the old Caledonian Forest that once clad much of the country. Here it is being allowed to regenerate naturally, and the resultant growth is fascinating. The wood runs up the steep slopes from Loch Maree, and the tracks give lovely glimpses of the loch cradled in the great hills.

If you follow the marked Nature Trail, you will find a very interesting Geological Plinth which shows very clearly the strange formation of these mountains. The lowest part of the plinth is grey Lewisian gneiss, which comes from the very foundations of our world. Above that is Torridonian Sandstone, a comparative newcomer, formed under ancient seas and baked in ancient deserts. The white cap is Cambrian Quartzite, a mere baby of 250 million years. Look closely at the quartzite and you will see faint tracks of tubular worms fossilised there. These were the very earliest forms of life to leave traces behind them: there was no life to leave traces when the sandstone and the gneiss were laid down. That plinth shows the geological make-up of these Torridonian mountains.

The Mountain Trail begins at the highest point of the Nature Trail, and if you follow that Mountain Trail you will climb to 1800 feet above the loch to the Conservation Cabin, and if you go beyond to the Conservation Cairn, you will be in a position to see thirty-one mountains of more than 3000 feet in one great majestic panorama encircling you. A wondrous sight, a sight of a magnificence most rare.

As you climb the Trail, the trees thin out as the exposure increases. It is easy to see where outcrops of limestone come to the surface, for there the heather ends and grass, with many flowers, grows brilliant green. There is a peculiar plateau there, of white quartzite, dotted with tiny lochans, and making a very strange, almost moon-like, landscape. There is a wealth of hardy Arctic plants here -- junipers, dewberry and mountain azalea.

The head of Loch Maree is a mile or so through Kinlochewe, and surely Loch Maree lives up to its reputation of being the finest of Scotland's fresh water lochs. For that title, of course, it competes with Loch Lomond and Loch Morar, but I feel that Loch Maree just squeezes past the post, perhaps because it is so much more accessible than Morar and so much quieter than Lomond.

The great white-capped mound of Slioch (3217feet) dominates the eastern end of the loch, but Slioch and the other high hills do not take anything from the beauty of Maree: they add to it in a composition of unequalled grandeur.

The loch is richly studded with islands, and one of them is Eilean Ma-ruibhe, sometimes called Isle Maree. The Irish saint Maol Rubha, who was buried at Applecross, had a cell on the island, and the loch is named for him. Eilean Ma-ruibhe was a place of pilgrimage for centuries, but today no trace remains of the saint's cell.

There is an old burial ground on the island, and two stones stand there, close together, each incised with a simple cross. They mark the resting place of two star-crossed lovers.

It all happened long ago, in the days of the Norsemen. There was a young Princess living on one of the islands in the loch, and she fell in love with a worthy young Prince, and he in love with her. In those days men had to travel far and fight hard, while women stayed home, doing the things women were held fitted to do. The Prince left on an expedition, swearing eternal love and fidelity, and was long away. When he returned at last, the first thing he saw on the loch was his Princess's barge, rowed along by her women, and on the barge a bier. It was his Princess. In despair and hopeless love he plunged his own dagger into his heart just as the barge reached the shore on which he stood. As he thrust at the dagger, the Princess rose from the bier shrieking in horror. She was not dead, of course, but merely testing his love. She grabbed the dagger, tore it from his dying body and thrust it into her own heart. Now the two lie together for eternity on Eilean Na Rubha, and one hopes they have found the happiness they sought.

It is just a legend, of course, and you don't have to believe it.

Perhaps you prefer the alternative legend about those two stones, which certainly exist, and are known as the Lovers of Loch Maree. According to this story, which also goes back to the old Norse days, Prince Olaf of Norway once had to spend the winter there, being unable to win back to Norway through the fierce winter gales. He met, and promptly fell in love with, Deora, the daughter of the King of Dalriada. She was staying on the Loch Maree island, guarded by a young warrior and an old man, her teacher. Of course, Deora also fell in love with Olaf.

On his way back to his camp one day, Olaf was waylaid by the young warrior, Hector Ruadh, or Red Hector, who, naturally and inevitably, was himself in love with Deora. Hector insisted that they duel for the lady. They did, and Olaf fell, and was left for dead. However, a passing hunter found him and took him back to Isle Maree, where Deora nursed him back to health. Hector, of course, had disappeared. One day the King called for his daughter, and she had to leave the island and her lover. Eventually Prince Olaf sent the old man to bring him news of her, arranging that when he returned he would signal his news from the shore, a red signal if all was well and a black if it was not. Weeks later, a black signal appeared on the shore, and the despairing Olaf slew himself with his dagger.

When Deora returned she found her lover dead and accused her old teacher of the foul deed. He promptly slew her, and then, throwing off his disguise, revealed himself as Red Hector. Deora's attendants attacked him but he escaped, and leaped into the loch and was never seen again, not as Red Hector at least, for he was changed into a water horse, a kelpie, which to this very day is responsible for the sudden storms and squalls which so often sweep over the loch.

Personally, I don't believe he was turned into a kelpie. But the two stones do stand there in the old burial ground of Isle Maree.

There was once a Holy Well on this island, too, now dried up. It was a well famous for curing the sick, especially those afflicted with madness. One day a man brought a mad dog there in the hope of a cure, and the spirit of the well obliged. However, the spirit was angry at being used to treat a dog, and so left the well and the island.

And that is not all, for there is also a Wishing Tree, now dead, but once very famous. For centuries people came here and draped the old holly tree in colourful cloths and pushed coins into its clefts, and wished. Queen Victoria did it, when she visited Loch Maree, but because the wishes had to be kept secret, we do not know whether the regal hopes came to pass.

It was in 1877 that the Queen visited Loch Maree and stayed at the Loch Maree Hotel, which is still there and still dispensing warmth and comfort to the traveller. A large engraved stone in the Hotel grounds records, in Gaelic, that:

Queen Victoria stayed six nights at Loch Maree Hotel and in her Gracious Condescension willed that this Stone should be a Remembrance of the pleasure she found in coming to this part of Ross-shire.

The Queen, also in her Gracious Condescension, allowed a nearby waterfall, which she visited, to be named Victoria Falls. The falls are up the hill above the loch, and there is a forest road and track to them, starting about 2 miles past the hotel. A visit there could well be an acceptable and gentle counterpoint after a strenuous day in the hills.

There is no road along the north-east shore of Loch Maree, but a track, for walkers only, does run along most of its length. That track runs under the great bulk of Slioch, but you can't really appreciate all the beauties of that mountain from close up.

About half way along the length of the loch is Furnace, a name which tells you about the place. This was the largest iron smelting plant in Scotland 350 years ago, although there is but little trace of it now. The works were built by Sir John Hay, starting in the very early 17th century, and they operated for twenty-five years. The earliest blast furnace in Scotland was built there. The smelting was done by charcoal, and to make the charcoal all the woods for many miles around were felled. Each furnace required about 3500 tons of wood a year, and the resulting denudation of the hills is to a large extent responsible for the barren beauty we admire today, and that is so not only of Loch Maree but of many other places in Scotland. It had taken many centuries, from the last Ice Age, for Scotland's ice-gouged land to grow its covering of trees, but it took only a few years to destroy that cover, and allow the thin soil to be washed off the hills. That wholesale felling of trees was one of the first examples of how Scotland's scarce natural resources have been raped and robbed repeatedly, leaving behind an empty, but very beautiful, desolation. Even the Clearances are an example of this.

As a matter of fact, the Government, then in Edinburgh, for it was before the Union, was concerned about the wholesale felling of trees, and tried to regulate it, but Sir John Hay was a powerful industrialist of his day (he later became the Earl of Kinnoul) and had no difficulty in circumventing the regulations.

Of course there was not a great deal of ore available in Scotland, except for some 'bog iron' found in the peat mosses, and eventually ore had to be imported from England. With that additional cost, and the increased cost of carrying charcoal greater distances as the local forests were cleared, the Scottish furnaces became less profitable, and were closed, leaving little trace behind them except, as here on Loch Maree, heaps of furnace slag.

THE SLIOCH

The road on the west side of Loch Maree leaves the loch side about half way along its length and heads off due west for Gairloch.

From just about where the road leaves the loch, a track goes off to the right and eventually reaches Poolewe. The track, which is the ancient Tollie Path, does not stick to the lochside, but climbs high above it, and gives very fine vistas of Loch Maree and its cradling mountains.

Loch Maree is without question one of the most memorable scenic experiences in all of Scotland: the Tollie Path shows it in all its glory. It is not a long walk -- perhaps six miles, although there are some hills to climb -- and it would make a fine afternoon for walkers, who could meet the transport again at Poolewe.

Before reaching Gairloch on the road, a minor road to the left heads off for Badachro, Erradale and Red Point. It is a *cul-de-sac* of course, like so many of these delightful roads to the peninsulas on the coast, but it is very pleasant indeed.

There is one particularly fine viewpoint just by Opinan where

the road overlooks a vast prospect of sea and islands, with Skye as an appropriate and distant frame for Rona and Raasay.

From Red Point, where the road ends, a foot track continues very finely right round the coast to link up with the road again at Diabaig on Loch Torridon. That makes a grand coastal walk on a summer's day, with fine beaches and the opportunity for lots of worthwhile beachcombing.

Gairloch village, at the head of Gair Loch (from the Gaelic *Gearr*, or 'Short'), has a fine open situation, and, unusually for these Highland villages, has excellent sandy beaches. It is still a fishing port, and that adds to the attractions, for those bound to the land are always fascinated by the trappings and activities of those whose living comes from hunting over the wild waters. Perhaps there is a little sea water in the veins of us all.

The views from Gairloch, and round about the village, are very fine. The Torridon mountains, Skye and even the Outer Hebrides are all paraded here, although perhaps the best views are found a mile or two along the road (A832) to Poolewe, where there is some height.

Most unusually for the north-west, Gairloch even has a golf course, although the views from the course are liable to be a considerable distraction. Sea angling, too, is a big attraction for many at Gairloch, and of course there is also an infinity of loch and burn fishing in the district for the enthusiast.

Gairloch also houses the local Heritage Museum, and there surely is no finer example of the small communally operated museums now so popular. When you visit it, and you really should, don't hurry inside, but take a few minutes to examine the exhibit of Highland flora at the entrance. Here are all the plants and herbs we so unthinkingly tread on whenever we walk the hills. They are beautiful and diverse, and seeing them displayed like this may well make us all more observant and even respectful.

Inside the museum is a large and very well displayed variety of exhibits, showing many aspects of life in the Highlands, today and in the past. There is even a reproduction of a croft house, and that is likely to dispel any misty and romantic notions about life in the not-so-distant past. There are exhibitions on fishing and agriculture, dyeing and spinning, and many other aspects of Highland life.

As with most of these small museums, the exhibits are not shown remotely in glass cases, but can be examined at close quarters and from all angles. It makes them so much more intimate.

There are also more ancient things, from the stone and bronze ages, and a truly magnificent Pictish carved stone showing a fish, still distinct and sharp after so many centuries. Altogether, the Gairloch Museum is an excellent place to visit, and cannot be recommended too strongly. There is a very good restaurant, too. You might even have a wet day during your Highland holiday, for that is not unknown: if so, there could be no bettter place to spend it than at this museum.

One of the nastiest little episodes of Scotland's blood-stained history took place at Flowerdale, just south of Gairloch. Flowerdale House still stands, and in a field just below the present house you can just make out where the old An Tigh Dige stood. It was a black house, and was surrounded by a moat.

The MacLeods of Gairloch lived there, and this was their country. About 1480, Alan McLeod was laird, and happily married to a daughter of the laird of Kintail, a sister of Hector Roy Mackenzie. They had two sons, fine growing lads. Alan had two brothers, who, for reasons not clear, hated all Mackenzies and were determined that no taint of Mackenzie blood should spoil the pure line of McLeod. One day the two found Alan sleeping in the heather. They struck off his head. That was on Cnoc na Miochanhairle, the Hill of Evil Counsel. The two then went to find the children, dragged them from their mother and slaughtered them, and then threw the blood-stained shirts of father and sons at their distraught Mackenzie mother.

She went off immediately to her father, Mackenzie of Seaforth, at Brahan Castle, and Mackenzie sent his brother and the blood-stained clothing to Edinburgh and the court of the King. The King rose in anger, and Commission of Fire and Sword was given to

Mackenzie against the McLeods. He took the commission, and executed it, not only against the murderers, but against all McLeods and decimated them with great slaughter.

In 1494 the brother of the dead Hector Roy received from the King the grant of all McLeod lands at Gairloch, for almost no McLeods were left, and the Mackenzies held those lands down the centuries.

A small side road (B8021) goes from Gairloch round the north side of the loch, then up the open sea as far as Melvaig, and from there a private track continues right up the coast to Rubha Reidh (Smooth Point), and the lighthouse there. Once more, this is a dead-end road, but the views it gives over the Minch, out to the Hebrides and back down to the Inner Sound and the Sound of Raasay are very fine. By following the coast from the lighthouse round the north of the peninsula, into Loch Ewe, you can reach another roadhead at Cove on the western side of Loch Ewe.

Keep your eyes open as you travel this track and you may be lucky. Somewhere hereabouts there is a keg of gold buried. It was gold belonging to the Jacobites, and was buried by one of Prince Charles Edward's men in 1746. The man who buried it was Duncan Macrae of Isle Ewe, and he was a wizard. Using the power of his black art he made the keg invisible, although it has to re-appear once every seven years. It was seen once by an old woman, years ago, and she marked the spot with her distaff, then hurried for help. When she returned, both distaff and keg of gold had disappeared. They have never been seen since, but just, the same, keep your eyes open.

The road north from Gairloch to Poolewe cuts across the neck of the peninsula, skirting Loch Tollaidh and through the village of Tollie and you can see where that Anglicised name came from. As already noted, there are grand views back over Loch Maree from this road.

The great attraction of Poolewe, of course, is the Inverewe Gardens there. They are such an attraction that well over 100,000 people visit them every year. Quite obviously, Inverewe is the end of the road for many Highland Tours, and the roads north of there are quite noticeably emptier than those further south -- not that the roads to the south are themselves particularly busy.

Inverewe is National Trust for Scotland property, and thus well-maintained and always open.

Over a hundred years ago Osgood Mackenzie determined to build a garden there, on a place known as Ploc Ard -- the High Lump. It was incredible, really, that he should have chosen that place, because it was a particularly barren bit of land, open to the vicious gales of the Minch, and almost devoid of soil. It was really nothing but a lump of Red Torridonian sandstone, and the little patches of soil were no more than acid black peat. There was some heather growing, and the only tree was a wind-stunted dwarf willow.

Osgood Mackenzie knew what he was about, though, and had a profound love of growing things. He knew also that the climate was mild, largely because of the Gulf Stream, that great mass of warmed water which inches its way from the coasts of South America right across the Atlantic and curls protectively round the west of Scotland.

After fencing that inhospitable lump of land, Mackenzie began by having soil brought in, in creels, and planted a wind break of pines and a hedge of the common purple rhododendron, which flourishes everywhere in the peat soil of this coast. Mackenzie recorded that it took four or five years before the pines started to grow, and twenty years before they were doing their job as a windbreak, but when they did, planting of more exotic species was begun. The emphasis was on Asian plants, and today there is an unequalled display of rhododendrons, azaleas, magnolias and hydrangeas, as well as quite magnificent trees from many parts of the world.

There are some startling contrasts, carefully arranged, with Himalayan lilies and forget-me-not-like plants from the South Sea islands blooming happily beneath Monterey pines and silver birches and palm trees.

It is grand at any time of year, but best in spring and early summer when the mass of colour sings like some great choir after the miles of subdued colours of moor and mountains.

This had long been Mackenzie country, and in his book *A Hundred Years in the Highlands* Osgood Mackenzie gives a remarkable picture of life in what was then a very remote and isolated part of the country. It is a record of a life that had changed little over many generations, and tells vividly of how the family took responsibility for the lives of all those around them. The book tells about the building of Inverewe, but perhaps because he never really thought about it in that way, it does not tell how the Mackenzies fought to keep clearances off their land, and to make an adequate life for the many people for whom they felt responsibility. There were no clearances in Gairloch, and the Mackenzies did whatever they could whenever they could to help the population by providing employment, lending money for boats and guaranteeing fish prices. The building of the garden, too, utilised a vast amount of labour, and provided security for many.

Osgood Mackenzie died in 1922, but his daughter carried on the work he had started, and then in 1952 the garden was handed over to the National Trust for Scotland. Go there, in spring if possible, but go there at any time and wander over those 2000 acres, enjoy the vistas and the distant views of sea and islands and mountains, and give thanks to a most remarkable man whose vision has brought great joy to many people.

From Inverewe the road, still A832, swings away northward up the east side of Loch Ewe and past the lovely Isle of Ewe, rich and fertile and green as a jewel just off shore by Aultbea, where there is still an Admiralty depot, for it was here in Loch Ewe that many of the great Atlantic convoys assembled for their hazardous journeys during the last war.

If you want to see more of Loch Ewe, and to see it without any of the traffic distraction of the quiet main road, then keep left at Aultbea, and carry on round the coast to the strangely named Mellon

Charles. It is yet another dead end road, of course, and only a couple
of miles of it, but the views over Loch Ewe and across to the
Gairloch peninsula are grand.

At Aultbea the main road leaves Loch Ewe and cuts across a
neck of land to Gruinard Bay. A minor road to the left just where
you reach the bay takes you, if you wish, up that tongue of land
between Loch Ewe and Gruinard Bay.

There is a very fine track leading off that road at Achgarve,
which will take you past loch and burn to the coast at lovely and
quite deserted Slaggan Bay. The views on that short stretch of road
from Aultbea to Laide are grand indeed, especially to the south and
east.

You are looking, of course, at another great empty quarter,
which runs for many miles through barren deer forests. Gruinard
Forest, Fisherfield Forest, Letterewe Forest, Dundonnell Forest,

Strathnasheallag Forest, Fannich Forest -- many square miles empty now of all human habitation, and given up to deer.

Just where the road reaches the bay at Laide are the faint remains of a very ancient chapel, and tradition maintains very strongly that it was built by St. Columba himself. Whether St. Columba or one of his followers, it was a very ancient building, and has been dated to the 7th century.

Gruinard Bay is unusual on this rockbound coast in having no fewer that three glorious beaches, with pink sand from the Torridon rocks. That pink sand in the Bay produces some of the most astonishing picture-postcard effects when the sea is blue and green and the hills bathed in bright sunshine. Photographs taken then are really rather hard to believe, especially if looked at by the fire on some winter night of driving sleet and blackness.

But there is a serpent in the Eden of Gruinard, and that is the island lying just off shore. That island was deliberately contaminated with anthrax during the last war, in experiments on germ warfare. Anthrax is a killer disease. The contamination would cease to be dangerous, so the scientists said, in another hundred years. Now we are assured that the danger is past, and that the island is safe. For me, at least, it will always carry the warning signs.

Leaving that obscenity behind, the road swings east again, and south, to go down the south-west side of Little Loch Broom. This is crofting country, and the road passes through several very typical crofting townships. In some of these the crofts are worked and productive; in others the hard-won land has reverted to rushes and heather. A sad sight.

Dundonnell is at the head of Little Loch Broom, and is a village dominated by the great ridge of An Teallach to the south. There is a large fish farm at Dundonnell, and it is interesting. Of course, there are fish farms now in almost all these west coast lochs, but this one welcomes visitors, and you can see the whole process there, from the tiny fingerling and fry to the trout ready for the pan. You can even feed some of the larger fish, and that is a clever piece of enterprise, for you buy the food from the farm to feed the farm's own fish! There surely can be few enterprises more profitable than that!

An Teallach, that great ridge of red rock to the south of Dundonnell, gets its name of 'The Forge' from the mists that so often drift like smoke around its peaks. There are eleven peaks in all, rising to the summit at Bidean a' Glas Thuill at 3451 feet. That great ridge stretches for over three miles, and if you have reached it, provides one of the most exhilarating walks in all of Scotland, and is not too difficult, so long as you are properly equipped for what is really an alpine expedition.

The track to the ridge is perhaps strenuous, but presents no problems to a reasonably fit walker, and the rewards are many, for the views are grand beyond words, and it is here that you are most likely to spot a golden eagle soaring away over the great precipice.

There is a path from Dundonnell to Sgurr Fiona, a stiff walk perhaps, but climaxed by the small lochan of Tol an Lochain lying in a wonderful horseshoe of high hills.

If you hesitate about walking the whole ridge, then that expedition to Sgurr Fiona will have given you a fair sample of the delights of An Teallach. Do, though, take care: equip yourself properly, and be sure to inform someone of your destination. You are in mountains there, and they can be harsh and unforgiving.

Beyond Dundonnell the road (A832) continues south-east over the emptiness of Dundonnell Forest, which is a deer forest, of course, and consequently treeless. It is a grand road, swooping and soaring very finely, reaching heights of over a thousand feet in places.

This was a 'Destitution Road', built in the middle of last century during the potato famines. There were no free lunches in those days, and to qualify for meagre handouts of meal, men had to put in a hard day's labour on the road. Women, too, received relief, but only if they produced a certain amount of spinning and knitting. Those who did not work hard enough received no meal. There were claims, too, that relief was often witheld from those who refused to give up their Catholic beliefs. The very old, the pregnant, and the crippled were given special consideration. They only had to produce half the labour of the able-bodied, but then they received only half rations anyway. There are many such Destitution Roads in Scotland, and many of the small piers in villages were also built at the same time and under the same conditions.

Braemore is another communications centre, with one road (A835) running south-east to Garve, and north to Ullapool and the other, the one we have now travelled, to Dundonnel. Which ever road you travel, it leads to some of Scotland's grandest scenery.

The Corrieshalloch Gorge is close by Braemore. A car park at the side of the road leads to a wooded path and the deep gorge, with the great Falls of Measach at its head. The gorge is about a mile long and 200 feet deep, a narrow cleft in the the hard rocks, cut originally by melt water from glaciers. The little stream which flows through it today seems somehow inadequate, but the enormous waterfall by which that little stream enters the gorge is very impressive indeed.

There is a suspension bridge over the falls, and it gives a rather stomach-churning view of both the falls and the gorge, which is clad in a richness of trees, lichens and ferns. Far from being gloomy, as one might expect, the gorge is very bright and colourful. Certainly something not to be missed.

Like so much else, it is carefully cherished by the National Trust for Scotland. The bridge over the gorge, incidentally, was built as 'a congenial amusement' by Sir John Fowler, who was also responsible for the Forth Railway Bridge, so even if it does sway around a little, you need not fear for its strength.

From Corrieshalloch the road, at last, heads straight to the north, towards Loch Broom and Ullapool.

Ullapool is a planned village. It did not just grow, Topsy-like, by chance, but was built and planned as a whole by the British Fisheries Society in 1788. The herring was the attraction; they shoaled in untold millions in Loch Broom and the adjacent waters.

There had been much fishing here for long before the Fisheries Society established itself, and there are traces of old curing stations here and there. But the Society brought big capital, and it was invested in a pier, storehouses, an inn and fishermen's houses.

There is a fascinating report in the First Statistical Account of Scotland of what happened when the herring shoals appeared:

People are instantly afloat with every species of sea-worthy craft....They press forward with utmost eagerness to the field of slaughter -- sloops, schooners, wherries, boats of all sizes, are to be seen constantly flying on the wings of the wind from creek to creek and from loch to loch, according as the varying reports of men, of the noisy flights of birds, or tumbling and spouting of whales and porpoises attract them....

It was too good to last, of course, and the herring were fished out after half a century. By the second half of the last century, Ullapool had gone into a deep depression, its very reason for existing vanished. But it is booming again today, and again with fishing, for improved boats and gear allow the working of other waters, far away, and there are also the great migrant shoals of mackerel to be exploited, for how long, no-one can predict, for there is as little thought of conservation now as in the 18th century.

Usually, for the present at least, there are several great East European factory ships in Loch Broom, buying the catch of local fishing vessels, and into the vast maw of those ships pours an unending stream of fish to feed the insatiable appetite of the land-locked European people. The crews of those ships often come ashore, just before their vessel is due to sail, and buy large amounts of gifts for their families -- chocolate and crisps seem to be favourites. Not surprisingly, they look like all sailors in all ports, men doing a hard and sometimes dangerous task in difficult conditions, and it is surely good that they have the opportunity of coming ashore and seeing just a little of a way of life and a society organised very differently from their own.

The major ferry for Lewis now runs from Ullapool twice daily, and that adds much to the bustle of the town. From here you can also join the intricate network of MacBraynes steamers that knit the islands together. Surely there can be few more satisfying ways of

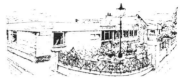
spending a vacation than island-hopping through the Hebrides on those steamers.

Ullapool is certainly a busy place, but equally certainly has not succumbed to the undoubted temptation of adopting the lowest common denominator of tourist traps. It is busy because it is a working port, and everything is subordinated to that. But it is an attractive town, well situated and organised.

For the visitor, there is much here. Sea-angling, especially, is a great attraction, and it is so good that several international competitions have been held. You can fish from the shore or from a boat, and if you are particularly ambitious, there is game fishing for the big ones, including shark.

There is not much of a beach at Ullapool -- it is all shingle -- but just north a mile or so at Ardmair there is a splendid beach, made all the more attractive by its backdrop of the great cliffs of Coigach towering up 2500 feet. Ardmair is also a place for collecting semi-precious stones from the beach. They are not always easy to recognise in their raw state (wet any possibles to check their colour), but amethysts, quartz of many kinds, cornelians and moss agates are quite common.

As for walking, you really can't do better than follow the tiny road up the Ullapool river and up Glen Achall, past Loch Achall and

away into the hills. Where the road ends, a track begins, and you can follow that eastwards, if you will, all the way to distant Oykel Bridge on the A837. It is a wild and lonely country, through the Rhidorroch Forest and Glen Einig, but it is walking of a rare grandeur.

There is a small museum at Ullapool, tucked away behind a bookshop. This is another community project, and it contains items of both local and general interest. It is a crammed little place, and some of the exhibits are somewhat bizarre, but very interesting, and when you visit it, as you should, do not forget to leave a donation, for museums like this depend on them.

Throughout all this part of the Highlands there are many National Trust for Scotland properties and National Nature Reserves. One cannot praise these places too highly: they do a most excellent job in preserving for our children some of the fragile beauties and wonders of the country. And they **are** fragile; even the highest and stoniest mountain can be changed and ruined by those who love it and visit it often.

And yet these oases of preservation are embedded in an area where everything is beauty, except for what has happened to the people. Of course lip service is paid to the necessity of keeping people alive in the Highlands and preserving the communities, but there is little practical effort, and the drift to the cities and the south continues, for there is as yet no alternative.

And still the agricultural land, the once fertile glens and straths, year by year go back to rushes and heather, and the croft houses bear a harvest of Bed and Breakfast signs, and the best crop a crofter can gather is a couple of caravans on the in-bye grazing.

It is time, and more than time, that as much attention be paid to the conservancy of people as the conservancy of nature.

CAPITAL 'E' FROM THE BOOK OF KELLS

LUATH PRESS

GUIDES TO

WESTERN SCOTLAND

SOUTH WEST SCOTLAND, Tom Atkinson. A guide book to the best of Kyle, Carrick, Galloway, Dumfries-shire, Kirkcudbrightshire and Wigtownshire. This lovely land of hills, moors and beaches is bounded by the Atlantic and the Solway. Steeped in history and legend, still unspoiled, it is not yet widely known. Yet it is a land whose peace and grandeur are at least comparable to the Highlands.

Legends, history and loving description by a local author make this an essential book for all who visit -- or live in -- the country of Robert Burns.

ISBN 0 946487 04 9. Paperback. £3:25p.

THE LONELY LANDS. Tom Atkinson. A guide book to Inveraray, Glencoe, Loch Awe, Loch Lomond, Cowal, the Kyles of Bute, and all of Central Argyll.

All the glories of Argyll are described in this book. From Dumbarton to Campbeltown there is a great wealth of beauty. It is a quiet and a lonely land, a land of history and legend, a land of unsurpassed glory. Tom Atkinson describes it all, writing with deep insight of the land he loves. There could be no better guide to its beauties and history. Every visitor to this country of mountains and lochs and lonely beaches will find that enjoyment is enhanced by reading this book.

ISBN 0 946847 10 3. Paperback. Price £3:25p.

THE EMPTY LANDS. Tom Atkinson. A guide book to the north of Scotland, from Ullapool to Bettyhill, and from Bonar Bridge to John O' Groats.

This is the fourth book in the series, and it covers that vast empty quarter leading up to the north coast. These are the Highlands of myth and legend, a land of unsurpassed beauty, where sea and mountain mingle in majesty and grandeur. As in his other books, the author is not content to describe the scenery (which is really beyond description) or advise you where to go. He does all that his usual skill and enthusiasm, but he also places that superb landscape into its historical context, and tells how it and the people who live there have become what we see today. With love and compassion, and some anger, he has written a book which should be read by everyone who visits or lives in -- or even dreams about -- that empty land.

ISBN 0 946487 13 8. Paperback. £3:25p.

HIGHWAYS AND BYWAYS IN MULL AND IONA. Peter Macnab. In this newly revised guidebook to Mull and Iona, Peter Macnab takes the visitor on a guided tour of the two islands. Born and grown up on Mull, he has an unparalleled knowledge of the island, and a great love for it. There could be no better guide than him to those two accessible islands of the Inner Hebrides, and no-one more able to show visitors the true Mull and Iona.

ISBN 0 946487 16 2. Paperback. £2:75p.

ALSO FROM LUATH PRESS

WALKS IN THE CAIRNGORMS. Ernest Cross. The Cairngorms are the highest uplands in Britain, and walking there introduces you to sub-arctic scenery found nowhere else. This book provides a selection of walks in a splendid and magnificent countryside -- there are rare birds, animals and plants, geological curiosities, quiet woodland walks, unusual excursions in the mountains. Ernest Cross has written an excellent guidebook to those things. Not only does he have an intimate knowledge of what he describes, but he loves it all deeply, and this shows.

ISBN 0 946487 09 X. Paperback. £2:75p.

SHORT WALKS IN THE CAIRNGORMS. Ernest Cross. A variety of shorter walks in the glorious scenery of the Cairngorms. It may be that you seek a stroll to the pub after dinner, or a half day on the high tops, or a guided two-hour walk round a loch. This book has them all, in profusion. You will be ably guided, and your guide will point out the most interesting sights and the best routes.

ISBN 0 946487 23 5. Paperback. £2:75p.

SCOTTISH SKIING HANDBOOK. Hilary Parke. Illustrated by Bill Smith. This book will not teach you how to ski, but it will tell you everything else you need to know about skiing in Scotland. Where to go, how to go, when to go, what to wear, what to carry, what to do -- it's all here, written by one who has skied all the Scottish hills for a long time now, and knows every mogul by name. Written with humour, and illustrated by the hilarious cartoons of Bill Smith, nevertheless the book is a very serious guide to all aspects of the Scottish ski scene. Even Big Wullie in his go-anywhere Suzuki could learn much from it.

ISBN 0 946487 20 0 Paperback. £3:95p.

MOUNTAIN DAYS AND BOTHY NIGHTS. Dave Brown and Ian Mitchell. The authors have climbed, walked and bothied over much of Scotland for many years. There could be no better guide to the astonishing variety of bothies, howffs and dosses on the Scottish hills. They were part of the great explosion of climbing in the Fifties and Sixties, and they write of this with first-hand knowledge, sympathy and understanding.

Fishgut Mac, Desperate Dan, Stumpy and the Big Yin may not be on the hills any more, but the bothies and howffs they used are still there. There was the Royal Bothy, paid for by the Queen herself after an encounter with a gang of anarchist, republican hill-climbing desperadoes. There was the Secret Howff, built under the very noses of the disapproving laird and his gamekeepers. There was the Tarff Hotel, with its Three Star A.A. rating. These, and many more, feature in this book, together with tales of climbs and walks in the days of bendy boots and no artificial aids.

ISBN 0 946487 15 4. Paperback. £5:95p.

TALES OF THE NORTH COAST. Alan Temperley and the pupils of Farr Secondary School. In this collection of 58 tales, there is a memorial to the great tradition of Highland story-telling. Simply told and unadorned, these tales are wide-ranging -- historical dramas, fairy tales, great battles, ship-wreck and ghosts, Highland rogues -- they all appear in this gallimaufry of tales, many of which have been told and re-told for generations round the fireside.

ISBN 0 946487 18 9 Paperback. £5:95.

POEMS TO BE READ ALOUD. *A Victorian Drawing Room Entertainment.* Selected and with an Introduction by Tom Atkinson. A very personal collection of poems specially selected for all those who believe that the world is full of people who long to hear you declaim such as these. The Entertainment ranges from an unusual and beautiful *Love Song* translated from the Sanskrit, to the drama of *The Shooting of Dan McGrew* and *The Green Eye of the Little Yellow God,* to the bathos of *Trees* and the outrageous bawdiness of *Eskimo Nell.* Altogether, a most unusual and amusing selection.

ISBN 0 946487 00 6. Paperback. £3:25p.

HIGHLAND BALLS AND VILLAGE HALLS. G.W. Lockhart. There is no doubt about Wallace Lockhart's love of Scottish country dancing, nor of his profound knowledge of it. Reminiscence, anecdotes, social commentary and Scottish history, tartan and dress, prose and verse, the steps of the most important dances -- they are all brought together to remind, amuse and instruct the reader in all facets of Scottish country dancing. Wallace Lockhart practices what he preaches. He grew up in a house where the carpet was constantly being lifted for dancing, and the strains of country dance music have thrilled him in castle and village hall. He is the leader of the well known *Quern Players*, and he composed the dance *Eilidh MacIain,* which was the winning jig in the competition held by the Edinburgh Branch of the Royal Scottish Country Dance Society to commemorate its sixtieth anniversary.

This is a book for all who dance or who remember their dancing days. It is a book for all Scots.

ISBN 0 96487 12 X Paperback. £3:95p.

THE CROFTING YEARS. Francis Thompson. A remarkable and moving study of crofting in the Highlands and Islands. It tells of the bloody conflicts a century ago when the crofters and their families faced all the forces of law and order, and demanded a legal status and security of tenure, and of how gunboats cruised the Western Isles in Government's classic answer. Life in the crofting townships is described with great insight and affection. Food, housing, healing and song are all dealt with. But the book is no nostalgic longing for the past. It looks to the future and argues that crofting must be carefully nurtured as a reservoir of potential strength for an uncertain future.

Frank Thompson lives and works in Stornoway. His life has been intimately bound up with the crofters, and he well knows of what he writes.

ISBN 0 946487 06 5. Paperback. £4:75p.

TALL TALES FROM AN ISLAND. Peter Macnab. These tales come from the island of Mull, but they could just as well come from anywhere in the Highlands and Islands. Witches, ghosts, warlocks and fairies abound, as do stories of the people, their quiet humour and their abiding wit. A book to dip into, laugh over, and enthuse about. Out of this great range of stories a general picture emerges of an island people, stubborn and strong in adversity, but warm and co-operative and totally wedded to their island way of life. It is a clear picture of a microcosmic society perfectly adapted to an environment that, in spite of its great beauty, can be harsh and unforgiving.

Peter Macnab was born and grew up on Mull, and he knows and loves every inch of it. Not for him the 'superiority' of the incomer who makes joke cardboard figures of the island people and their ways. He presents a rounded account of Mull and its people.

ISBN 0 946487 07 3. Paperback. £5:95p.

BARE FEET AND TACKETY BOOTS. Archie Cameron. The author is the last survivor who those who were born and reared on the island of Rhum in the days before the First World War, when the island was the private playground of a rich absentee landowner. Archie recalls all the pleasures and pains of those days. He writes of the remarkable characters, not least his own father, who worked the estate and guided the Gentry in their search for stags and fish. The Gentry have left ample records of their time on the island, but little is known of those who lived and worked there. Archie fills this gap. He recalls the pains and pleasures of his boyhood. Factors and Schoolmasters, midges and fish, deer and ducks and shepherds, the joys of poaching, the misery of MacBraynes' steamers -- they are all here.

This book is an important piece of social history, but, much more, it is a fascinating record of a way of life gone not so long ago, but already almost forgotten.

ISBN 0 946487 17 0. Paperback. £5:95p

Any of these books can be obtained from your bookseller, or, in case of difficulty, please send price shown, plus £1 for post and packing, to:

LUATH PRESS LTD.

BARR, AYRSHIRE. KA26 9TN